In the autumn of 1835, General Don Antonio Lopez de Santa Anna dissolves the Federalist government of Mexico and places all governmental control into his own hands... Later that fall, colonists and insurgents arise in revolt at the abolishment of the 1824 constitution, first at Gonzales and later at San Antonio de Béxar... Determined to rid his country of the pirates, Santa Anna presses an army north and arrives in Béxar on February 23, 1836, carrying a flag of No Quarter...

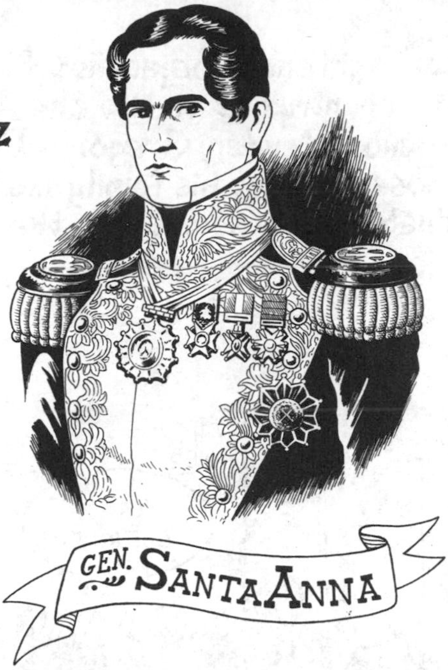
GEN. SANTA ANNA

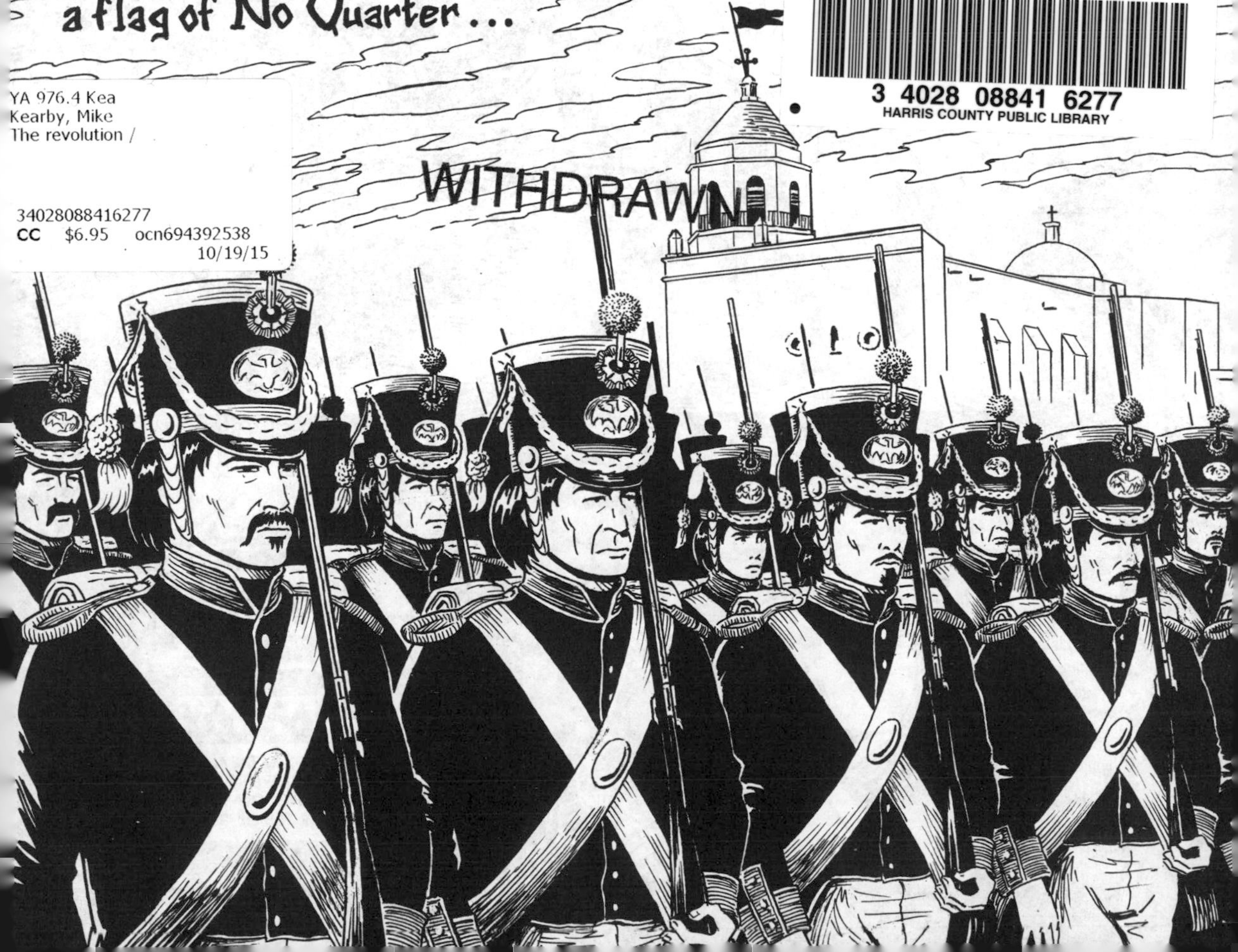

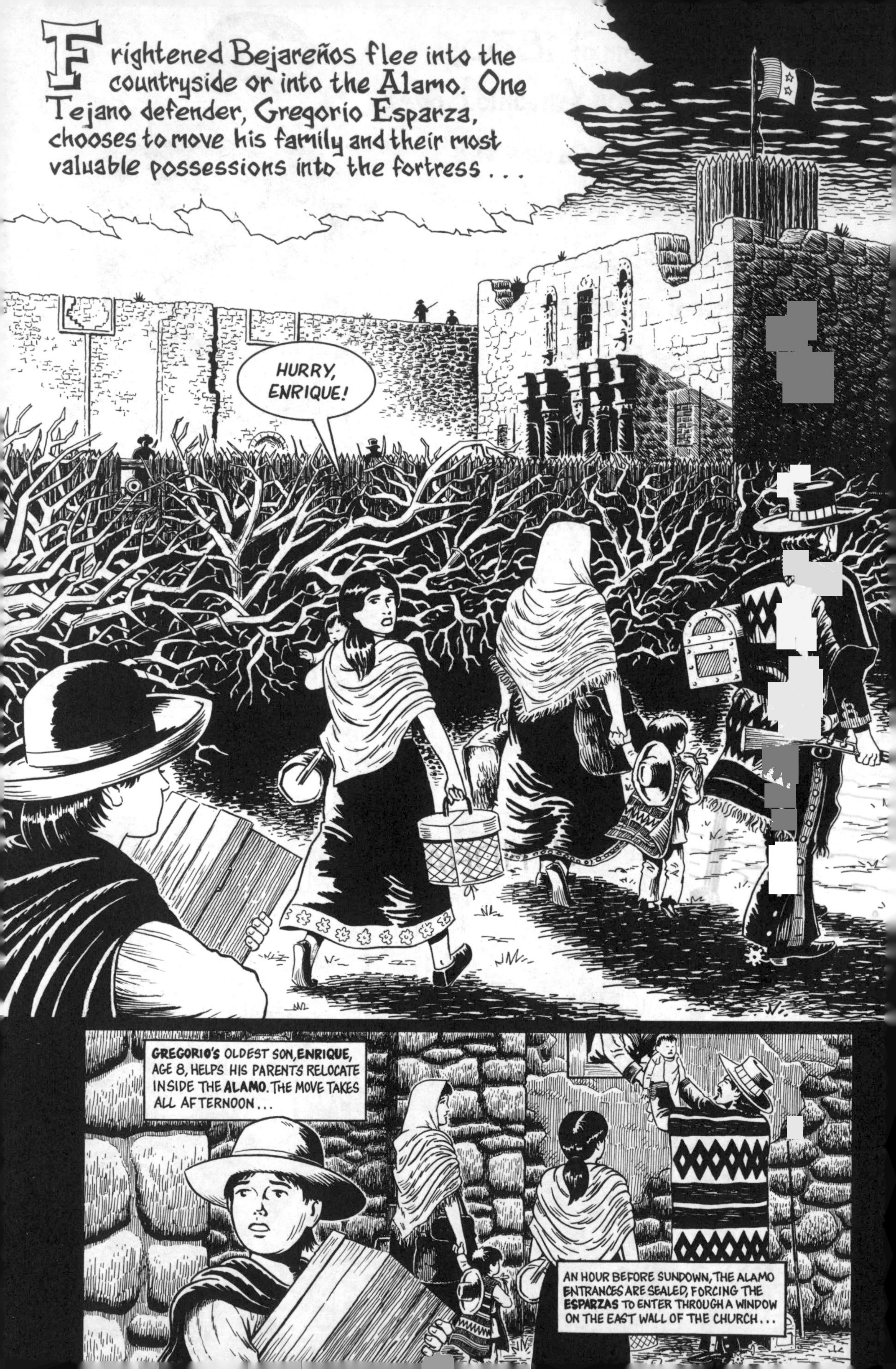
Frightened Bejareños flee into the countryside or into the Alamo. One Tejano defender, Gregorio Esparza, chooses to move his family and their most valuable possessions into the fortress . . .
HURRY, ENRIQUE!
GREGORIO'S OLDEST SON, ENRIQUE, AGE 8, HELPS HIS PARENTS RELOCATE INSIDE THE ALAMO. THE MOVE TAKES ALL AFTERNOON...
AN HOUR BEFORE SUNDOWN, THE ALAMO ENTRANCES ARE SEALED, FORCING THE ESPARZAS TO ENTER THROUGH A WINDOW ON THE EAST WALL OF THE CHURCH...

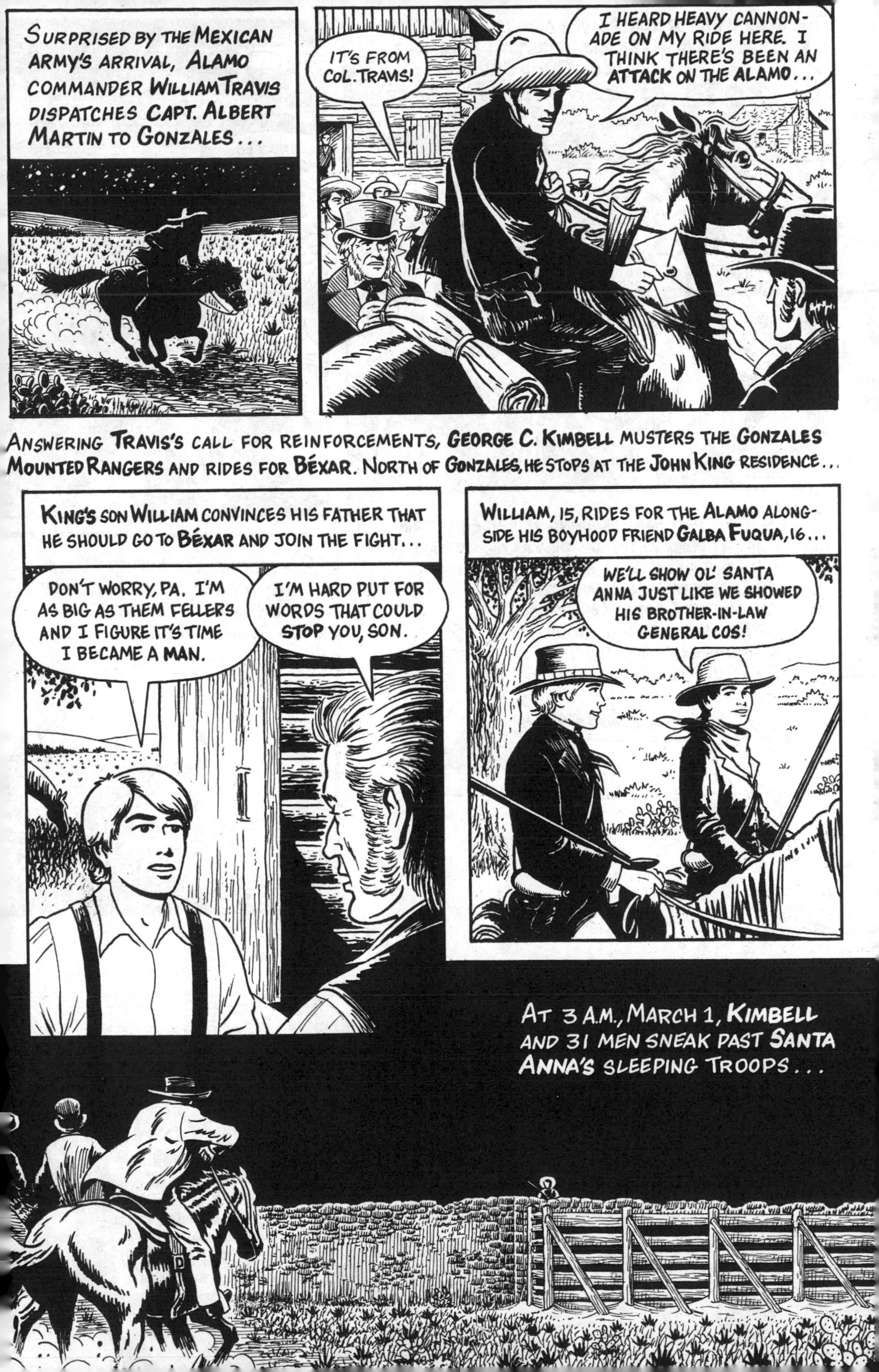
SURPRISED BY THE MEXICAN ARMY'S ARRIVAL, ALAMO COMMANDER WILLIAM TRAVIS DISPATCHES CAPT. ALBERT MARTIN TO GONZALES...
IT'S FROM COL. TRAVIS!
I HEARD HEAVY CANNONADE ON MY RIDE HERE. I THINK THERE'S BEEN AN ATTACK ON THE ALAMO...
ANSWERING TRAVIS'S CALL FOR REINFORCEMENTS, GEORGE C. KIMBELL MUSTERS THE GONZALES MOUNTED RANGERS AND RIDES FOR BÉXAR. NORTH OF GONZALES, HE STOPS AT THE JOHN KING RESIDENCE...
KING'S SON WILLIAM CONVINCES HIS FATHER THAT HE SHOULD GO TO BÉXAR AND JOIN THE FIGHT...
DON'T WORRY, PA. I'M AS BIG AS THEM FELLERS AND I FIGURE IT'S TIME I BECAME A MAN.
I'M HARD PUT FOR WORDS THAT COULD STOP YOU, SON.
WILLIAM, 15, RIDES FOR THE ALAMO ALONGSIDE HIS BOYHOOD FRIEND GALBA FUQUA, 16...
WE'LL SHOW OL' SANTA ANNA JUST LIKE WE SHOWED HIS BROTHER-IN-LAW GENERAL COS!
AT 3 A.M., MARCH 1, KIMBELL AND 31 MEN SNEAK PAST SANTA ANNA'S SLEEPING TROOPS...

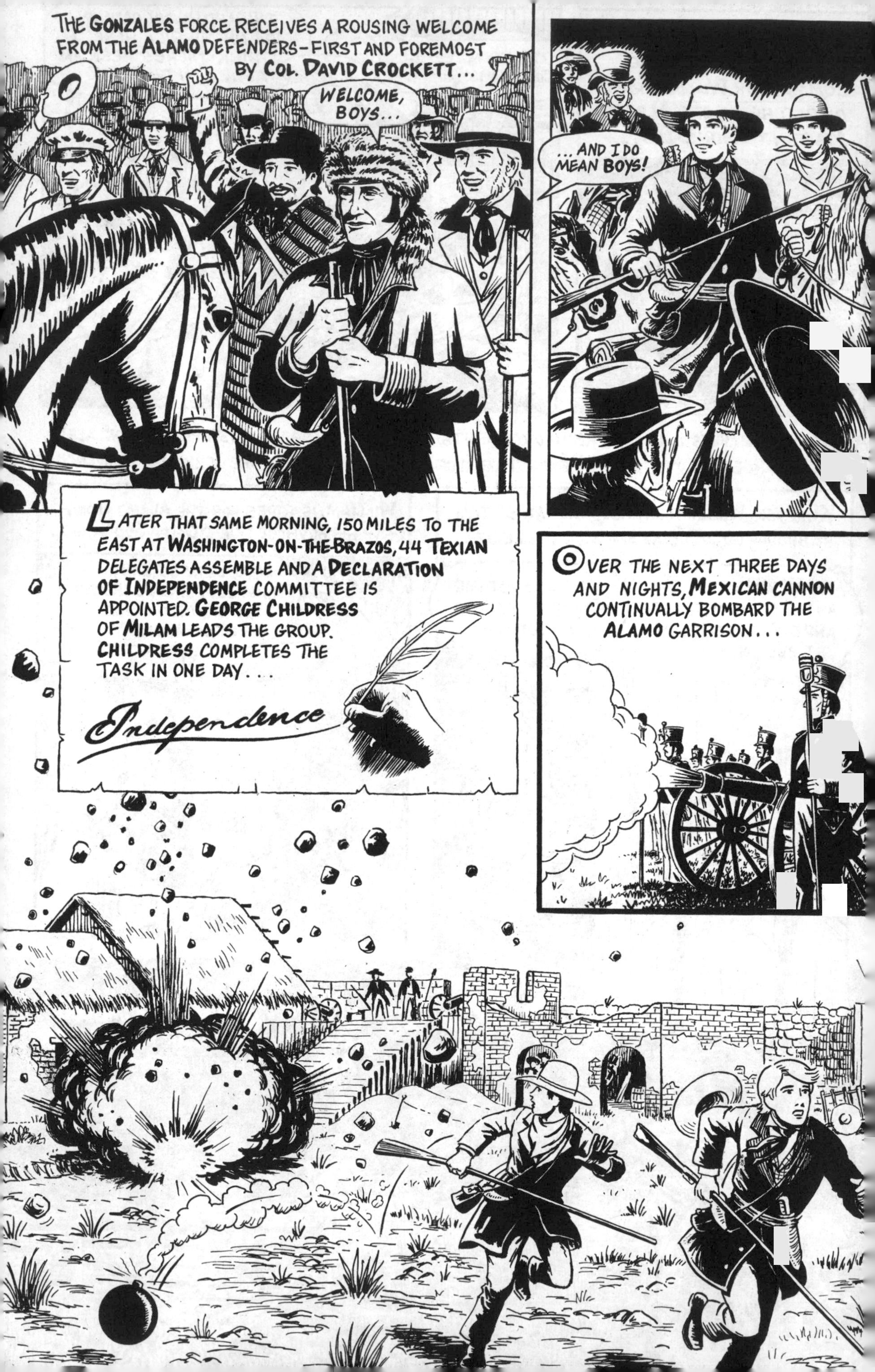
THE GONZALES FORCE RECEIVES A ROUSING WELCOME FROM THE ALAMO DEFENDERS–FIRST AND FOREMOST BY COL. DAVID CROCKETT...
WELCOME, BOYS...
...AND I DO MEAN BOYS!
LATER THAT SAME MORNING, 150 MILES TO THE EAST AT WASHINGTON-ON-THE-BRAZOS, 44 TEXIAN DELEGATES ASSEMBLE AND A DECLARATION OF INDEPENDENCE COMMITTEE IS APPOINTED. GEORGE CHILDRESS OF MILAM LEADS THE GROUP. CHILDRESS COMPLETES THE TASK IN ONE DAY...
Independence
OVER THE NEXT THREE DAYS AND NIGHTS, MEXICAN CANNON CONTINUALLY BOMBARD THE ALAMO GARRISON...

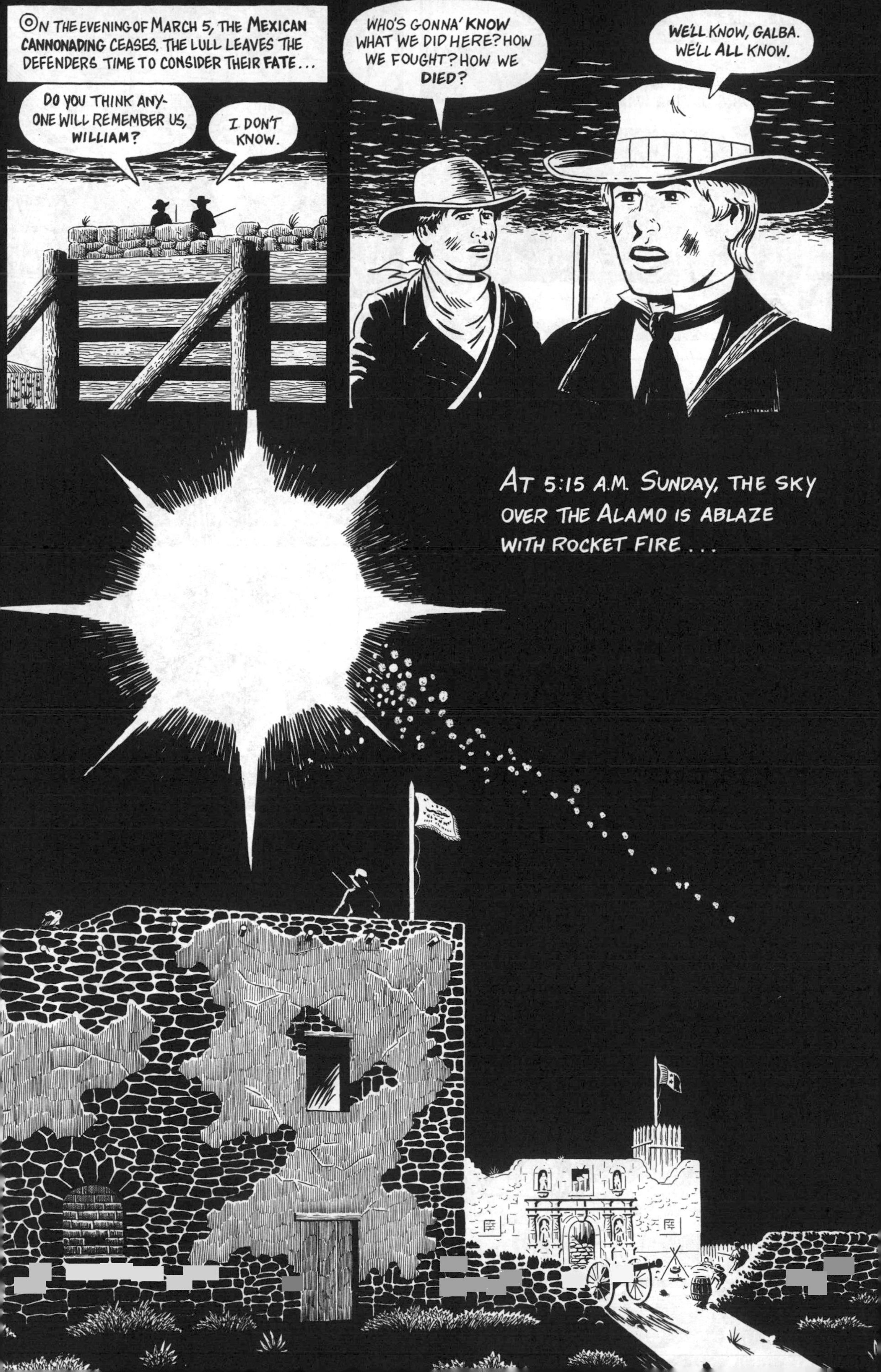
ON THE EVENING OF MARCH 5, THE MEXICAN CANNONADING CEASES. THE LULL LEAVES THE DEFENDERS TIME TO CONSIDER THEIR FATE . . .
DO YOU THINK ANYONE WILL REMEMBER US, WILLIAM?
I DON'T KNOW.
WHO'S GONNA' KNOW WHAT WE DID HERE? HOW WE FOUGHT? HOW WE DIED?
WE'LL KNOW, GALBA. WE'LL ALL KNOW.
AT 5:15 A.M. SUNDAY, THE SKY OVER THE ALAMO IS ABLAZE WITH ROCKET FIRE . . .

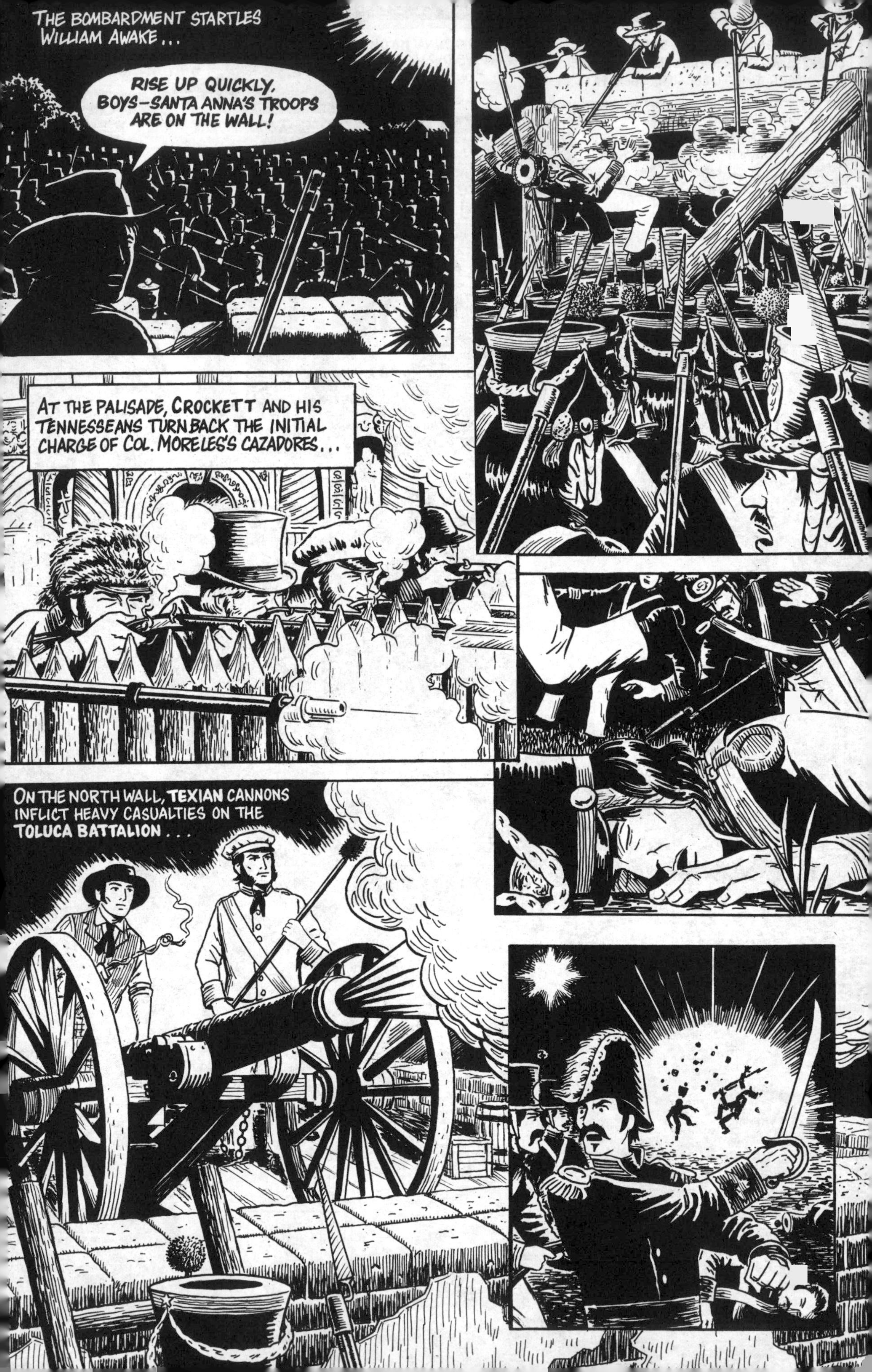
THE BOMBARDMENT STARTLES WILLIAM AWAKE...
RISE UP QUICKLY, BOYS—SANTA ANNA'S TROOPS ARE ON THE WALL!
AT THE PALISADE, CROCKETT AND HIS TENNESSEANS TURN BACK THE INITIAL CHARGE OF COL. MORELES'S CAZADORES...
ON THE NORTH WALL, TEXIAN CANNONS INFLICT HEAVY CASUALTIES ON THE TOLUCA BATTALION...

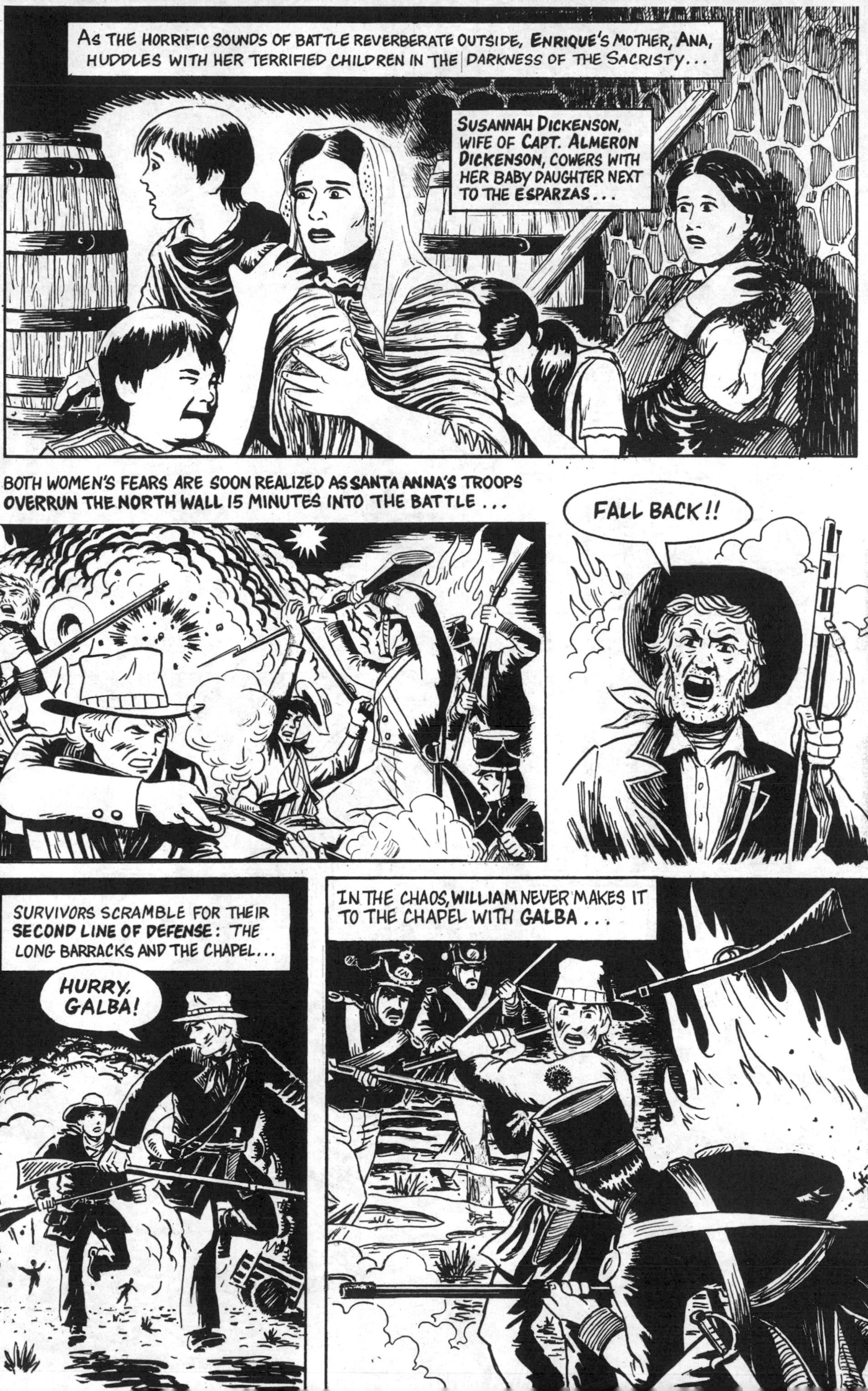

AS THE HORRIFIC SOUNDS OF BATTLE REVERBERATE OUTSIDE, ENRIQUE'S MOTHER, ANA, HUDDLES WITH HER TERRIFIED CHILDREN IN THE DARKNESS OF THE SACRISTY...
SUSANNAH DICKENSON, WIFE OF CAPT. ALMERON DICKENSON, COWERS WITH HER BABY DAUGHTER NEXT TO THE ESPARZAS...
BOTH WOMEN'S FEARS ARE SOON REALIZED AS SANTA ANNA'S TROOPS OVERRUN THE NORTH WALL 15 MINUTES INTO THE BATTLE...
FALL BACK!!
SURVIVORS SCRAMBLE FOR THEIR SECOND LINE OF DEFENSE: THE LONG BARRACKS AND THE CHAPEL...
HURRY, GALBA!
IN THE CHAOS, WILLIAM NEVER MAKES IT TO THE CHAPEL WITH GALBA...

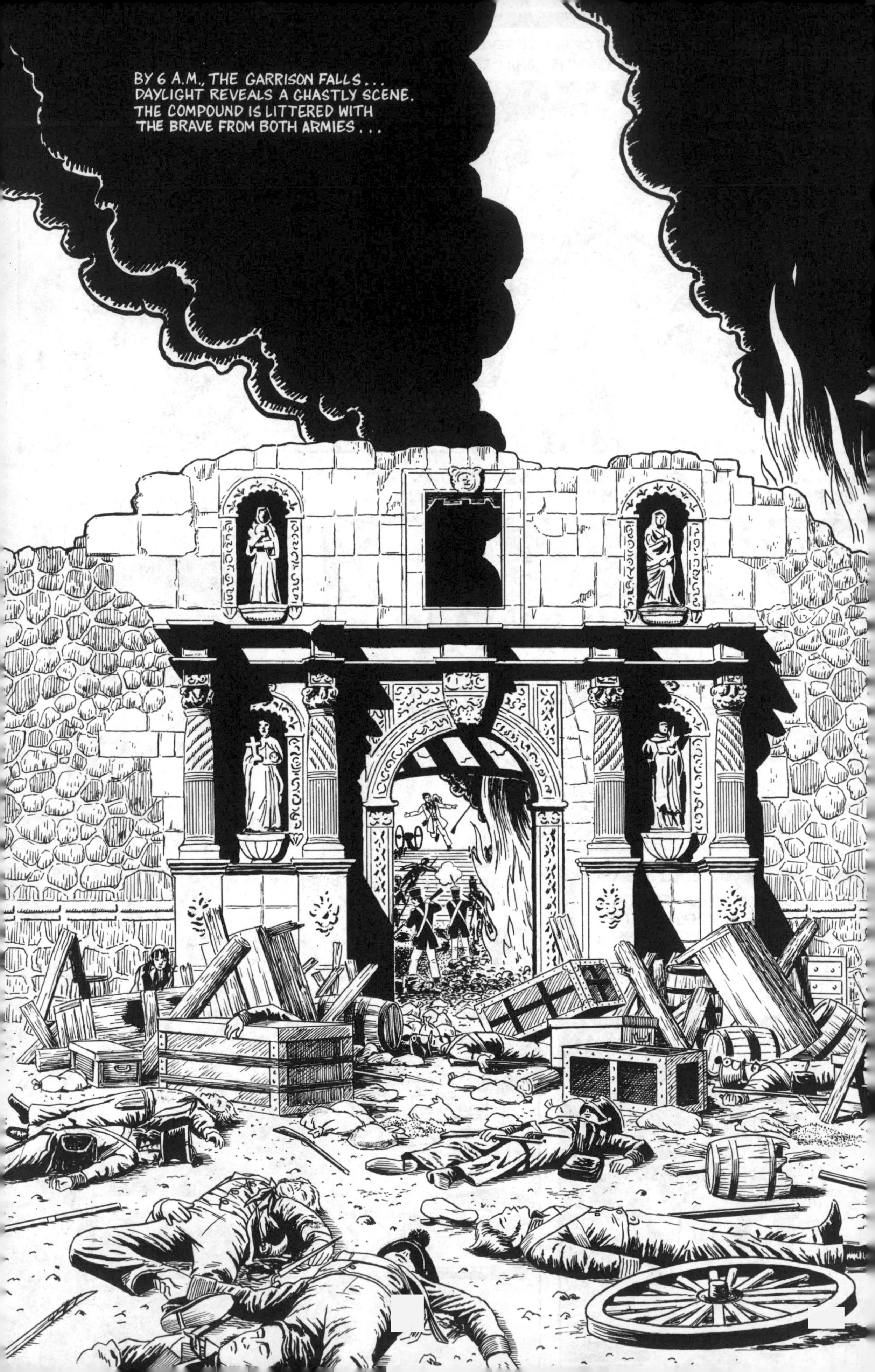
BY 6 A.M., THE GARRISON FALLS... DAYLIGHT REVEALS A GHASTLY SCENE. THE COMPOUND IS LITTERED WITH THE BRAVE FROM BOTH ARMIES...

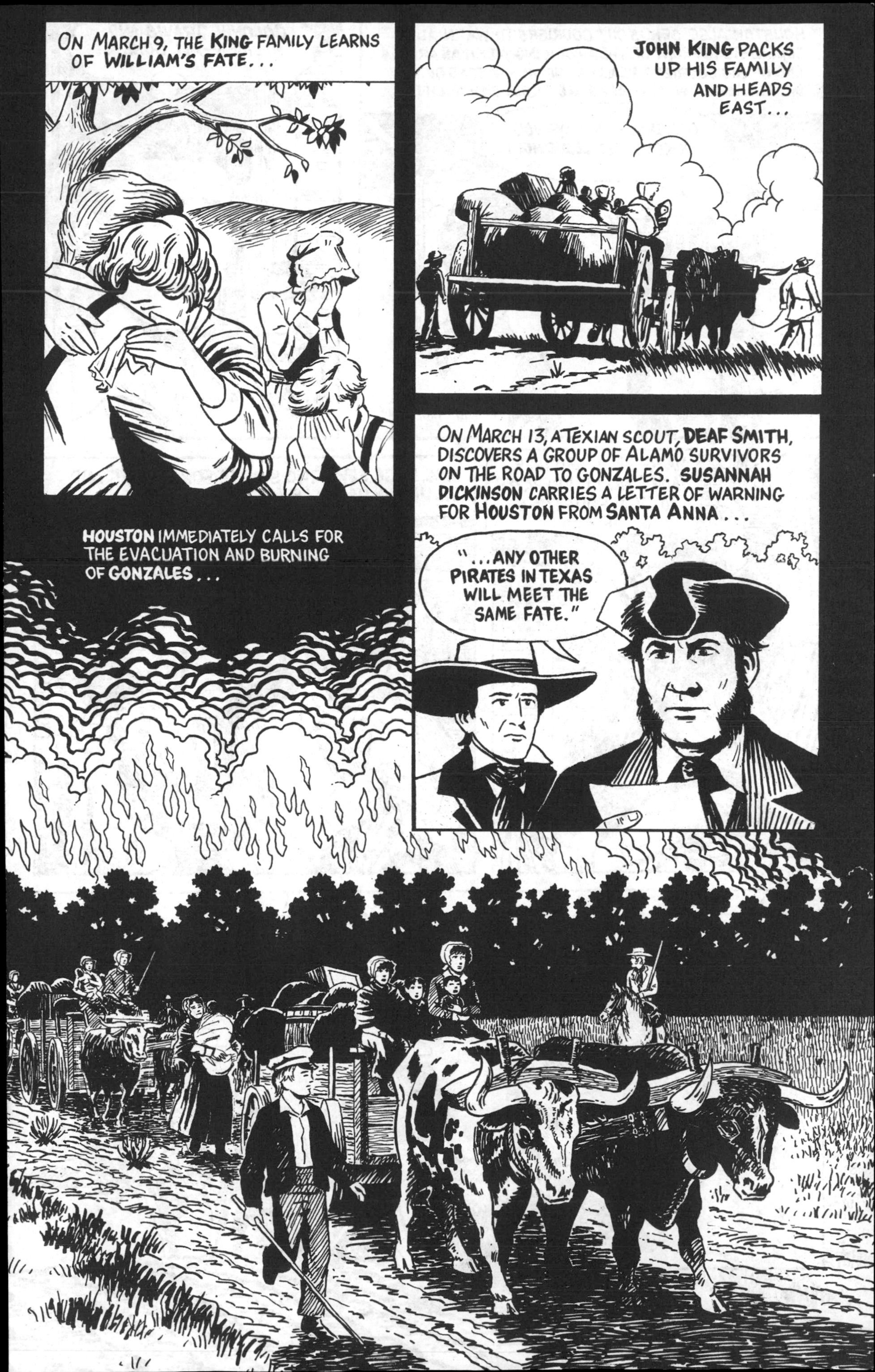

ON MARCH 9, THE KING FAMILY LEARNS OF WILLIAM'S FATE...
JOHN KING PACKS UP HIS FAMILY AND HEADS EAST...
ON MARCH 13, A TEXIAN SCOUT, DEAF SMITH, DISCOVERS A GROUP OF ALAMO SURVIVORS ON THE ROAD TO GONZALES. SUSANNAH DICKINSON CARRIES A LETTER OF WARNING FOR HOUSTON FROM SANTA ANNA...
"...ANY OTHER PIRATES IN TEXAS WILL MEET THE SAME FATE."
HOUSTON IMMEDIATELY CALLS FOR THE EVACUATION AND BURNING OF GONZALES...

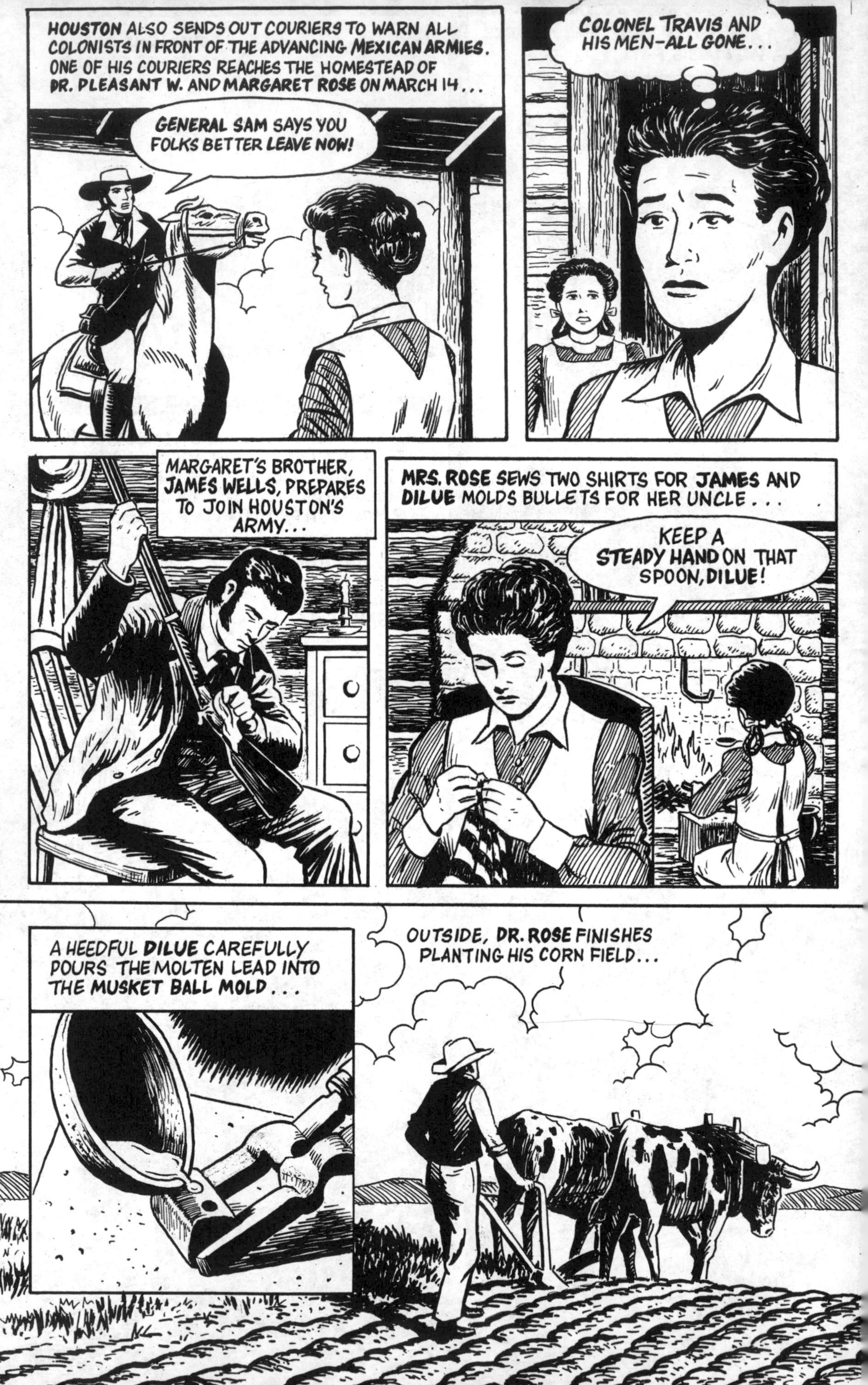
HOUSTON ALSO SENDS OUT COURIERS TO WARN ALL COLONISTS IN FRONT OF THE ADVANCING MEXICAN ARMIES. ONE OF HIS COURIERS REACHES THE HOMESTEAD OF DR. PLEASANT W. AND MARGARET ROSE ON MARCH 14...
GENERAL SAM SAYS YOU FOLKS BETTER LEAVE NOW!
COLONEL TRAVIS AND HIS MEN–ALL GONE...
MARGARET'S BROTHER, JAMES WELLS, PREPARES TO JOIN HOUSTON'S ARMY...
MRS. ROSE SEWS TWO SHIRTS FOR JAMES AND DILUE MOLDS BULLETS FOR HER UNCLE...
KEEP A STEADY HAND ON THAT SPOON, DILUE!
A HEEDFUL DILUE CAREFULLY POURS THE MOLTEN LEAD INTO THE MUSKET BALL MOLD...
OUTSIDE, DR. ROSE FINISHES PLANTING HIS CORN FIELD...

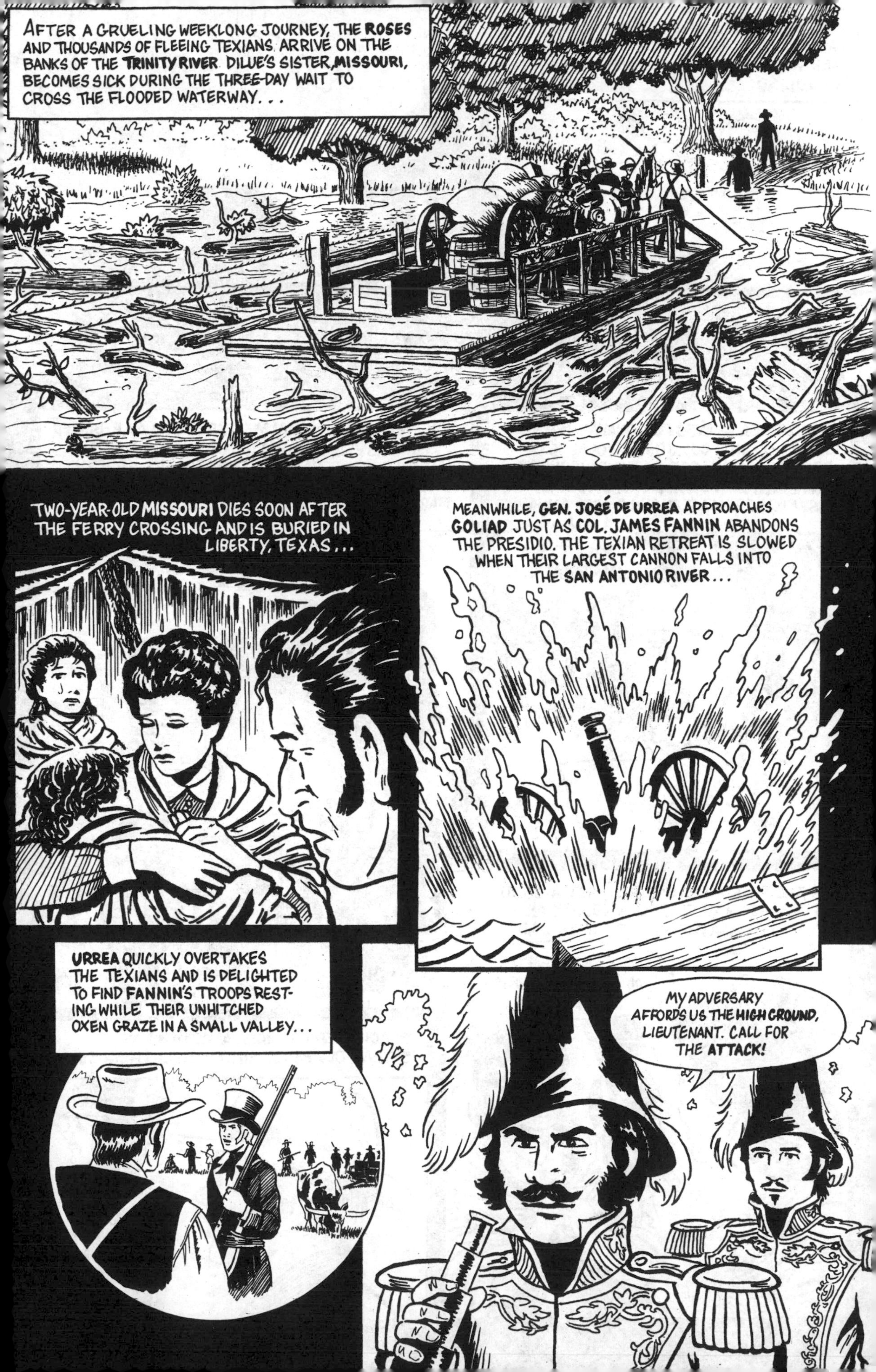
AFTER A GRUELING WEEKLONG JOURNEY, THE ROSES AND THOUSANDS OF FLEEING TEXIANS ARRIVE ON THE BANKS OF THE TRINITY RIVER. DILUE'S SISTER, MISSOURI, BECOMES SICK DURING THE THREE-DAY WAIT TO CROSS THE FLOODED WATERWAY...
TWO-YEAR-OLD MISSOURI DIES SOON AFTER THE FERRY CROSSING AND IS BURIED IN LIBERTY, TEXAS...
MEANWHILE, GEN. JOSÉ DE URREA APPROACHES GOLIAD JUST AS COL. JAMES FANNIN ABANDONS THE PRESIDIO. THE TEXIAN RETREAT IS SLOWED WHEN THEIR LARGEST CANNON FALLS INTO THE SAN ANTONIO RIVER...
URREA QUICKLY OVERTAKES THE TEXIANS AND IS DELIGHTED TO FIND FANNIN'S TROOPS RESTING WHILE THEIR UNHITCHED OXEN GRAZE IN A SMALL VALLEY...
MY ADVERSARY AFFORDS US THE HIGH GROUND, LIEUTENANT. CALL FOR THE ATTACK!

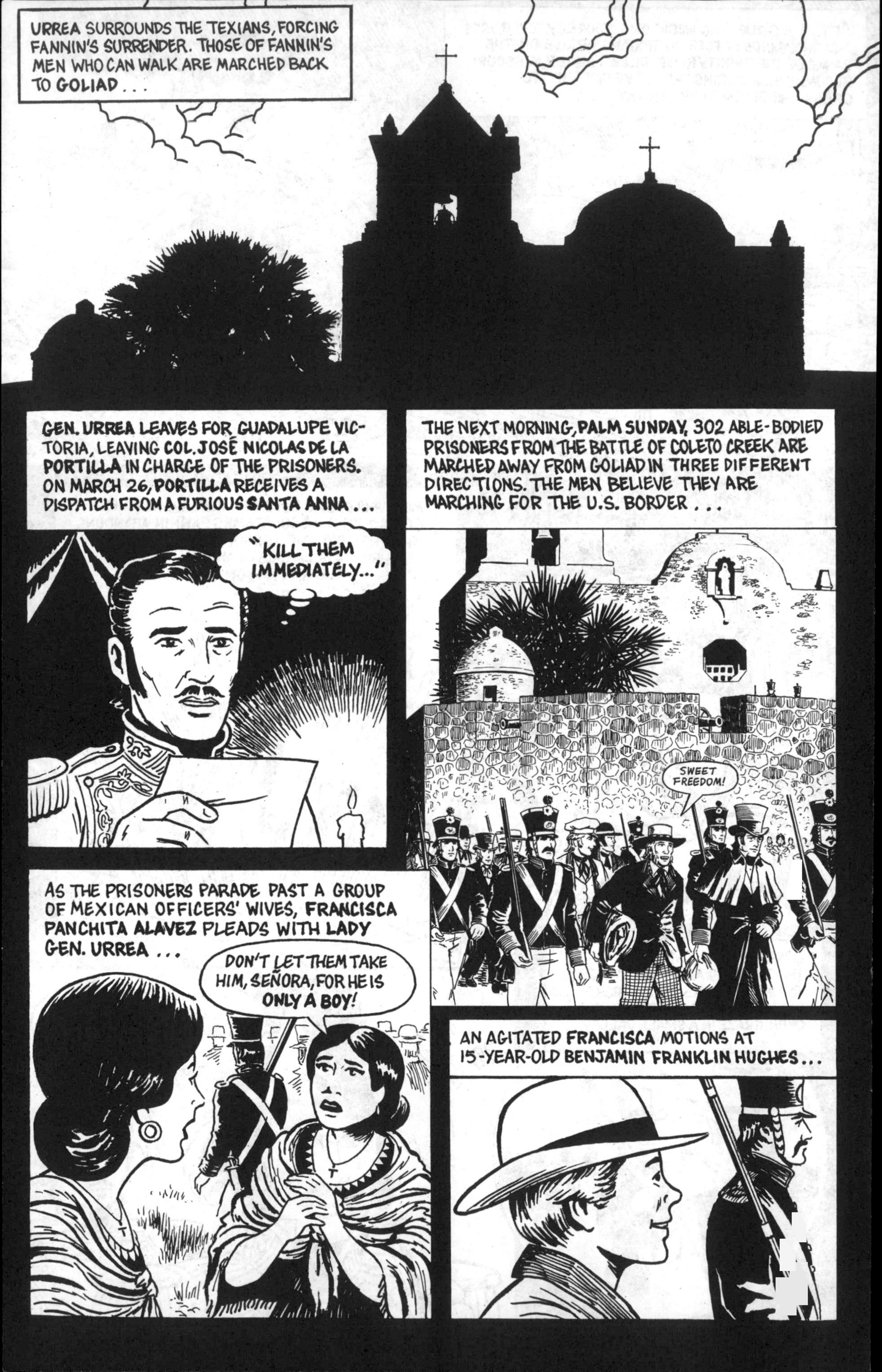
URREA SURROUNDS THE TEXIANS, FORCING FANNIN'S SURRENDER. THOSE OF FANNIN'S MEN WHO CAN WALK ARE MARCHED BACK TO GOLIAD . . .
GEN. URREA LEAVES FOR GUADALUPE VICTORIA, LEAVING COL. JOSÉ NICOLAS DE LA PORTILLA IN CHARGE OF THE PRISONERS. ON MARCH 26, PORTILLA RECEIVES A DISPATCH FROM A FURIOUS SANTA ANNA . . .
"KILL THEM IMMEDIATELY..."
THE NEXT MORNING, PALM SUNDAY, 302 ABLE-BODIED PRISONERS FROM THE BATTLE OF COLETO CREEK ARE MARCHED AWAY FROM GOLIAD IN THREE DIFFERENT DIRECTIONS. THE MEN BELIEVE THEY ARE MARCHING FOR THE U.S. BORDER . . .
SWEET FREEDOM!
AS THE PRISONERS PARADE PAST A GROUP OF MEXICAN OFFICERS' WIVES, FRANCISCA PANCHITA ALAVEZ PLEADS WITH LADY GEN. URREA . . .
DON'T LET THEM TAKE HIM, SEÑORA, FOR HE IS ONLY A BOY!
AN AGITATED FRANCISCA MOTIONS AT 15-YEAR-OLD BENJAMIN FRANKLIN HUGHES . . .

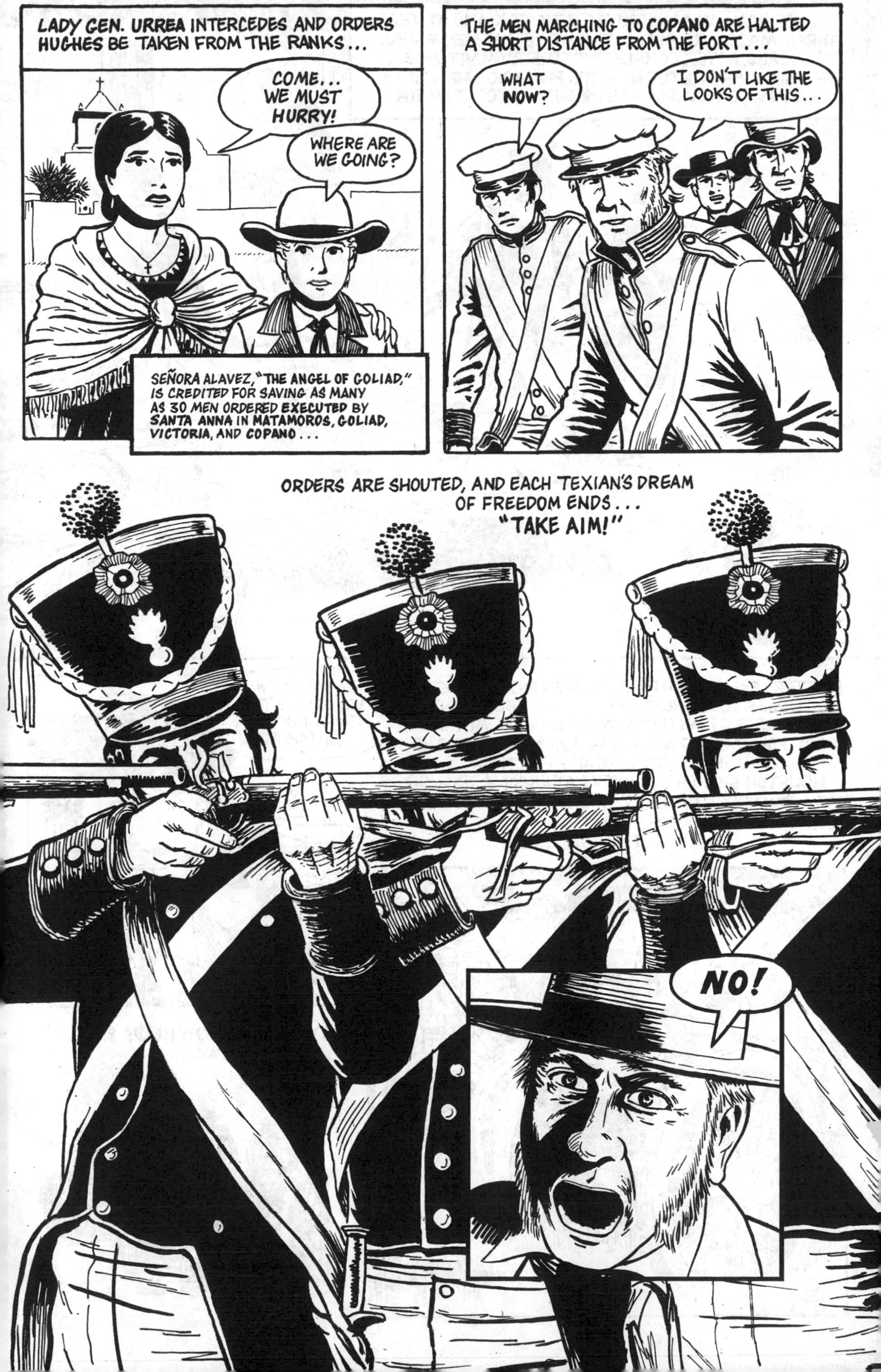
LADY GEN. URREA INTERCEDES AND ORDERS HUGHES BE TAKEN FROM THE RANKS...
COME... WE MUST HURRY!
WHERE ARE WE GOING?
SEÑORA ALAVEZ, "THE ANGEL OF GOLIAD," IS CREDITED FOR SAVING AS MANY AS 30 MEN ORDERED EXECUTED BY SANTA ANNA IN MATAMOROS, GOLIAD, VICTORIA, AND COPANO...
THE MEN MARCHING TO COPANO ARE HALTED A SHORT DISTANCE FROM THE FORT...
WHAT NOW?
I DON'T LIKE THE LOOKS OF THIS...
ORDERS ARE SHOUTED, AND EACH TEXIAN'S DREAM OF FREEDOM ENDS...
"TAKE AIM!"
NO!

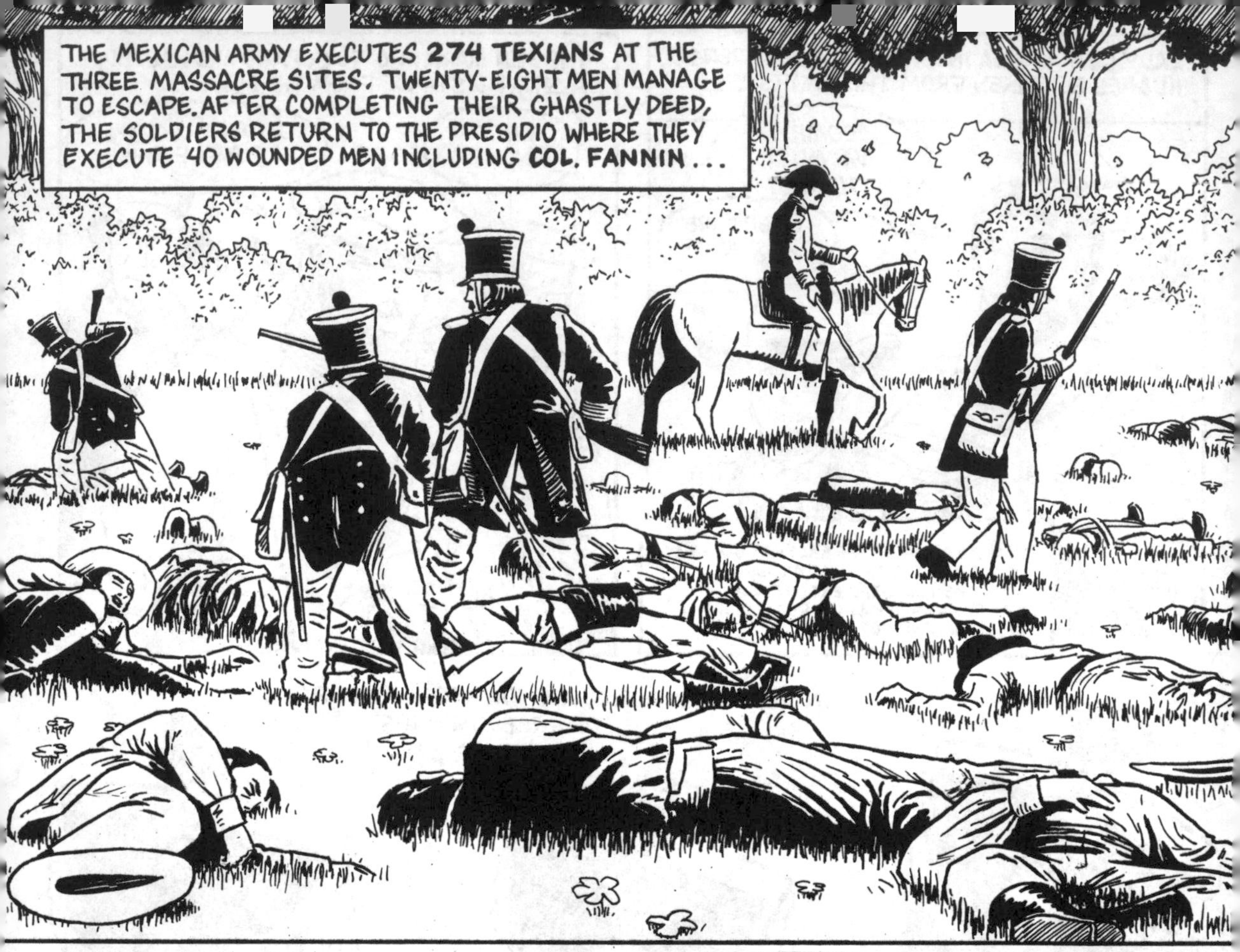
THE MEXICAN ARMY EXECUTES 274 TEXIANS AT THE THREE MASSACRE SITES. TWENTY-EIGHT MEN MANAGE TO ESCAPE. AFTER COMPLETING THEIR GHASTLY DEED, THE SOLDIERS RETURN TO THE PRESIDIO WHERE THEY EXECUTE 40 WOUNDED MEN INCLUDING COL. FANNIN...

AFTER LEARNING OF **FANNIN'S** SURRENDER, **HOUSTON** CONTINUES TO RETREAT EAST TO **SAN FELIPE** AND THEN **GROCE'S PLANTATION** ON THE **BRAZOS**. MUTINY SOON FOLLOWS AND AS MANY AS **300 MEN** LEAVE THE ARMY, REFUSING TO RETREAT ANY FURTHER...
←**HOUSTON** SPENDS TWO WEEKS AT **GROCE'S** DRILLING THE REMAINDER OF HIS ARMY. ON APRIL 11, TWO GIFTS FROM THE CITIZENS OF **OHIO** ARRIVE...
THE TWIN SISTERS...

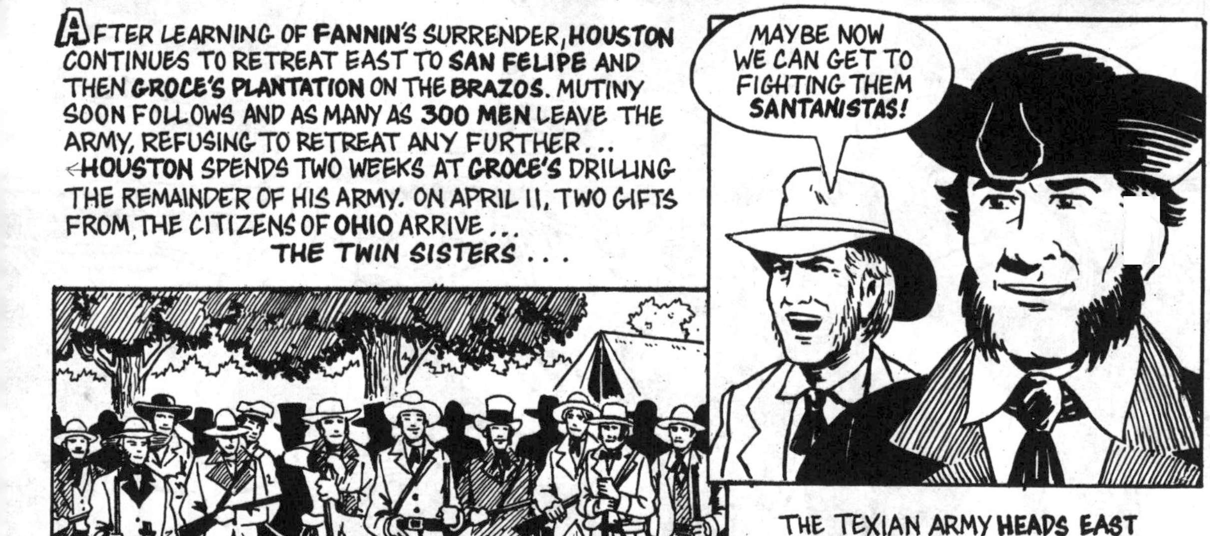
MAYBE NOW WE CAN GET TO FIGHTING THEM SANTANISTAS!

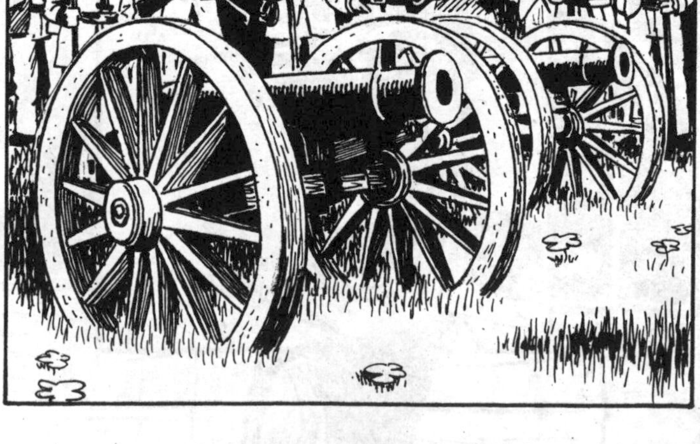

THE TEXIAN ARMY **HEADS EAST** THE NEXT DAY...

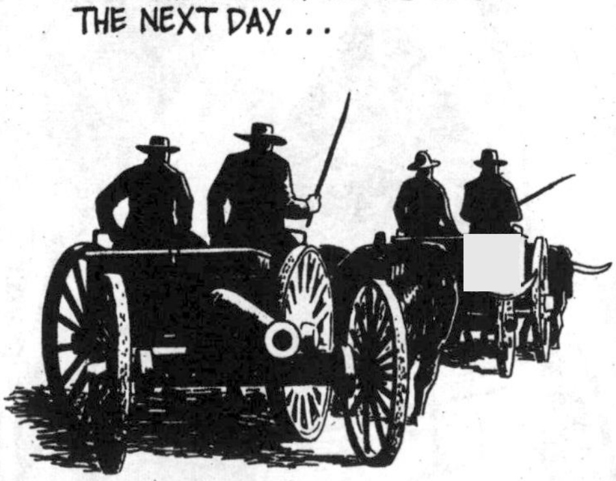

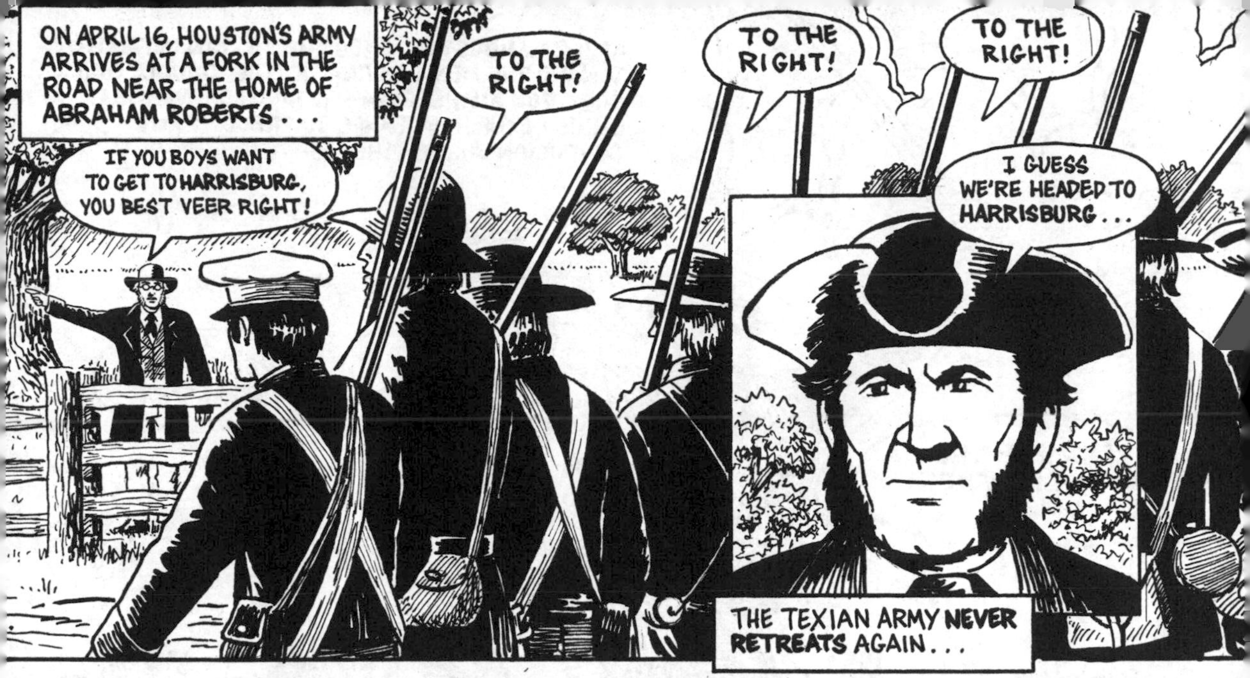
ON APRIL 16, HOUSTON'S ARMY ARRIVES AT A FORK IN THE ROAD NEAR THE HOME OF ABRAHAM ROBERTS . . .
IF YOU BOYS WANT TO GET TO HARRISBURG, YOU BEST VEER RIGHT!
TO THE RIGHT!
TO THE RIGHT!
TO THE RIGHT!
I GUESS WE'RE HEADED TO HARRISBURG . . .
THE TEXIAN ARMY NEVER RETREATS AGAIN . . .

BY APRIL 20, HOUSTON AND SANTA ANNA HAVE THEIR TROOPS IN PLACE AT SAN JACINTO. HOUSTON CALLS A COUNCIL OF WAR ON APRIL 21. ONLY TWO TEXIAN OFFICERS FAVOR AN ATTACK. HOWEVER, HOUSTON HAS ALREADY FORMULATED HIS PLAN AND SENDS DEAF SMITH TO DESTROY VINCE'S BRIDGE . . .

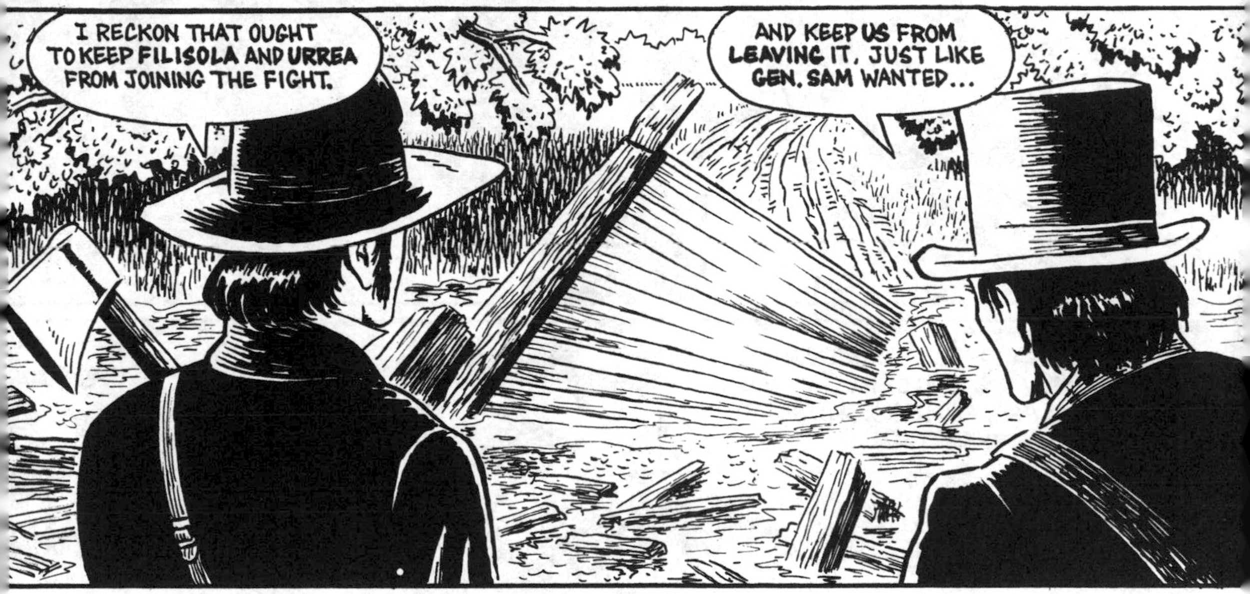
I RECKON THAT OUGHT TO KEEP FILISOLA AND URREA FROM JOINING THE FIGHT.
AND KEEP US FROM LEAVING IT, JUST LIKE GEN. SAM WANTED . . .

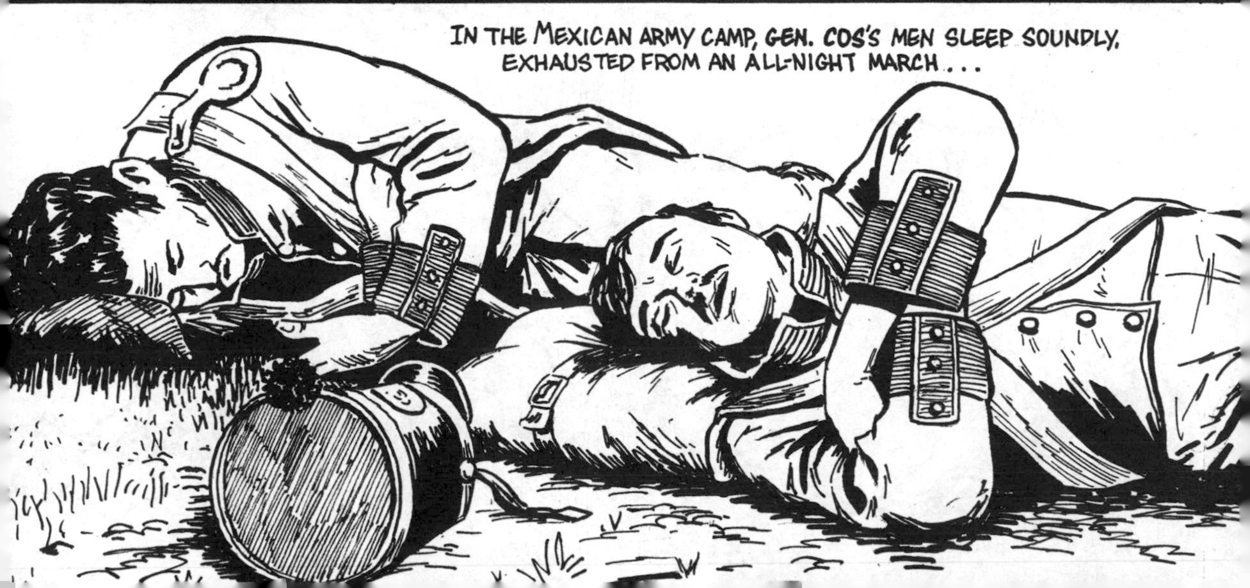
IN THE MEXICAN ARMY CAMP, GEN. COS'S MEN SLEEP SOUNDLY, EXHAUSTED FROM AN ALL-NIGHT MARCH . . .

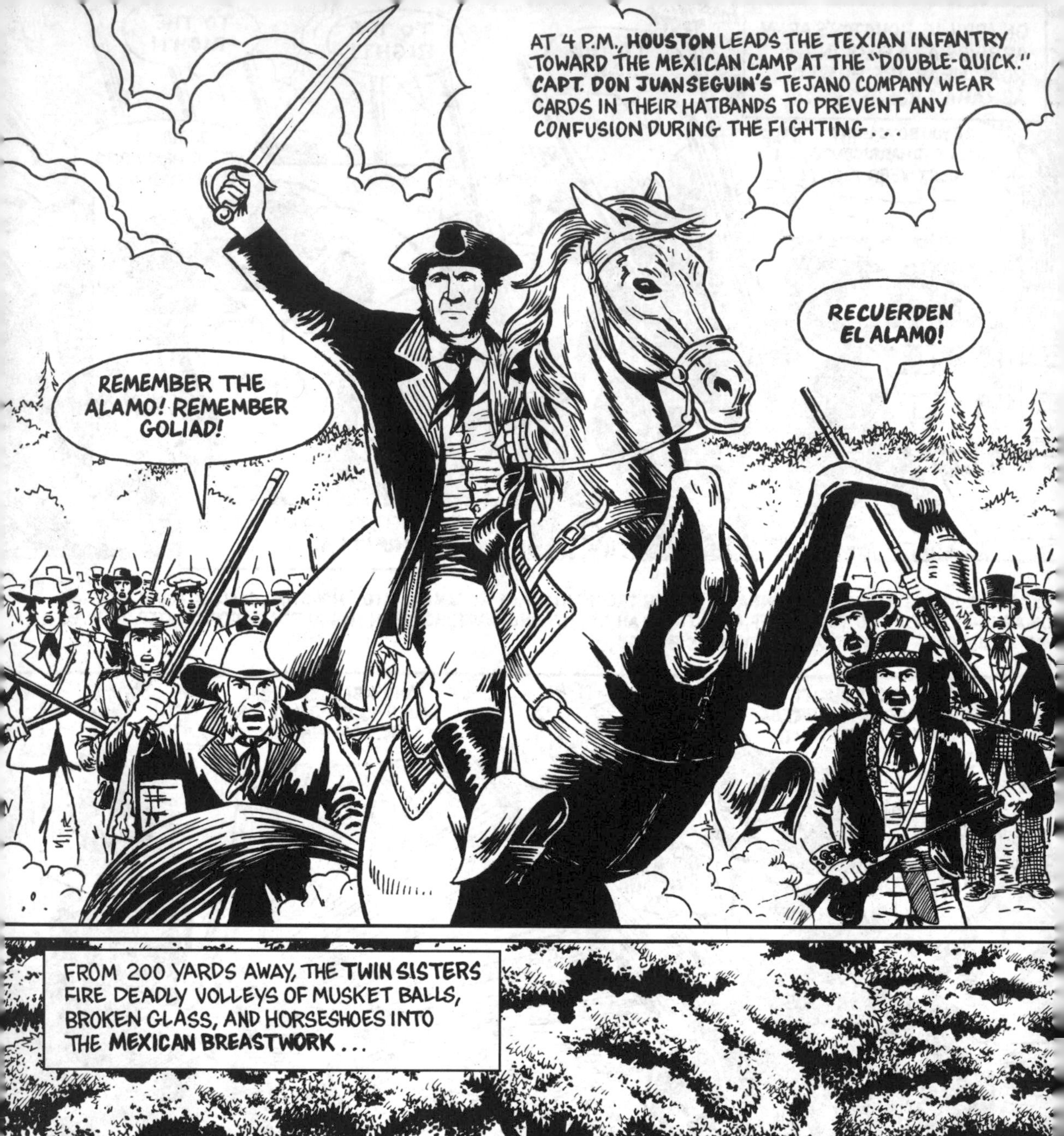
AT 4 P.M., HOUSTON LEADS THE TEXIAN INFANTRY TOWARD THE MEXICAN CAMP AT THE "DOUBLE-QUICK." CAPT. DON JUAN SEGUIN'S TEJANO COMPANY WEAR CARDS IN THEIR HATBANDS TO PREVENT ANY CONFUSION DURING THE FIGHTING . . .
REMEMBER THE ALAMO! REMEMBER GOLIAD!
RECUERDEN EL ALAMO!

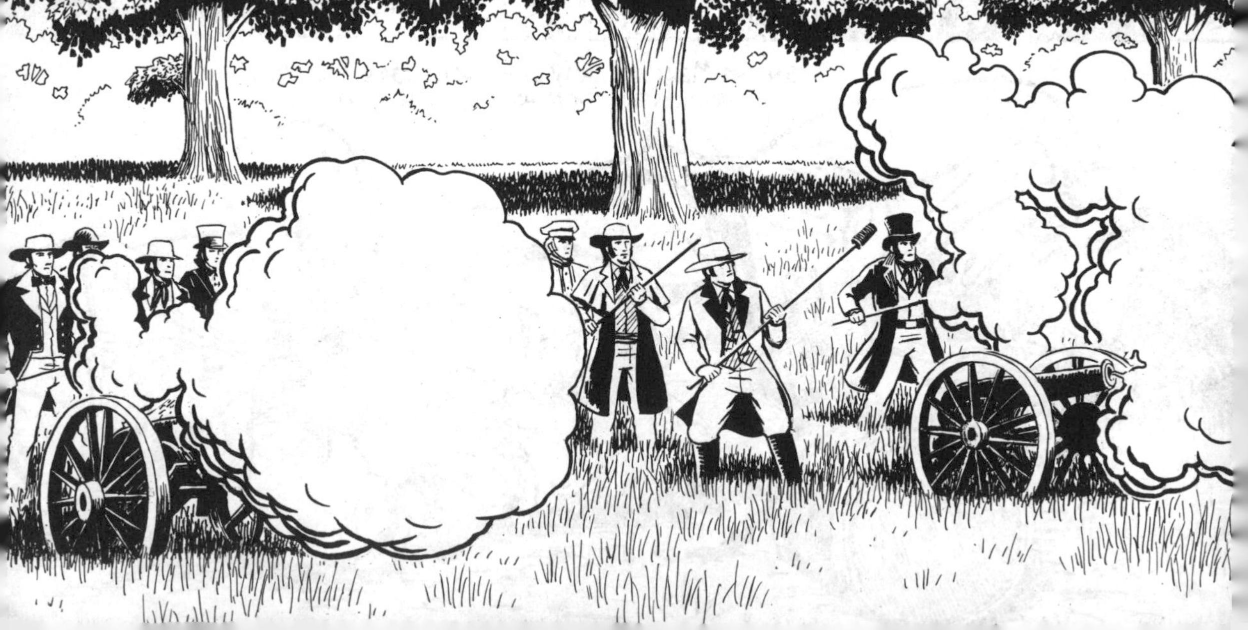
FROM 200 YARDS AWAY, THE TWIN SISTERS FIRE DEADLY VOLLEYS OF MUSKET BALLS, BROKEN GLASS, AND HORSESHOES INTO THE MEXICAN BREASTWORK . . .

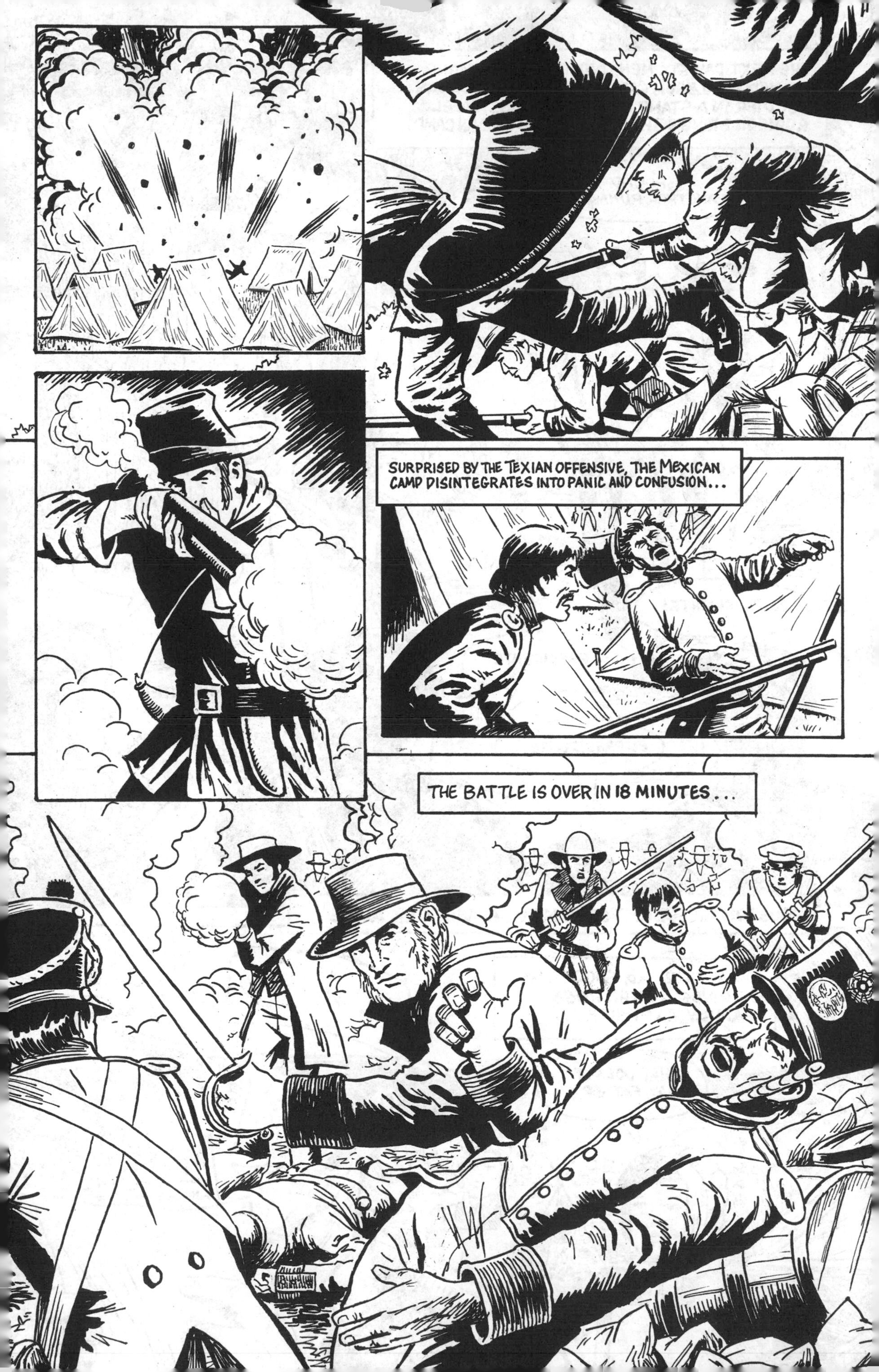
SURPRISED BY THE TEXIAN OFFENSIVE, THE MEXICAN CAMP DISINTEGRATES INTO PANIC AND CONFUSION...
THE BATTLE IS OVER IN 18 MINUTES...

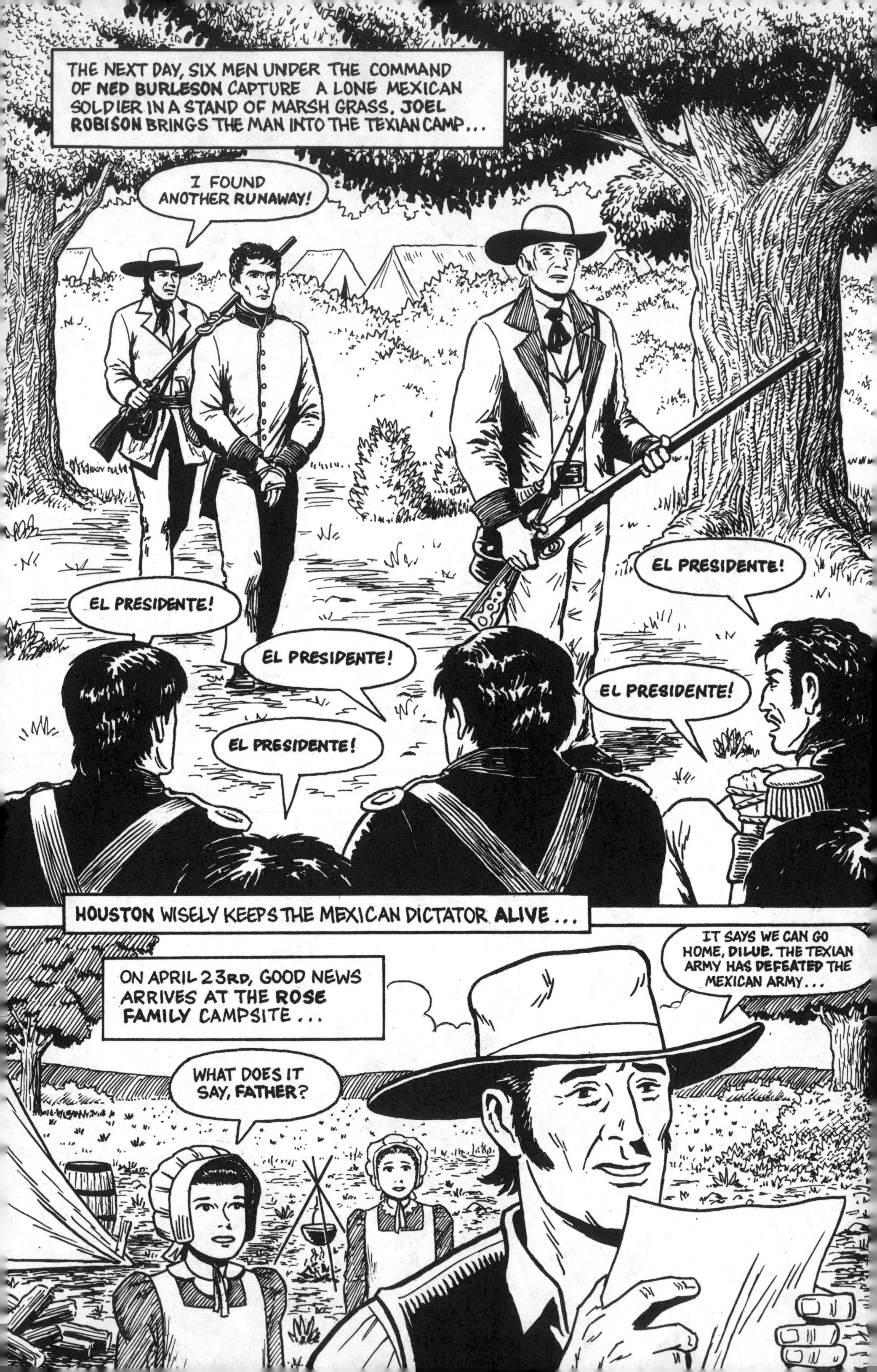
THE NEXT DAY, SIX MEN UNDER THE COMMAND OF NED BURLESON CAPTURE A LONE MEXICAN SOLDIER IN A STAND OF MARSH GRASS. JOEL ROBISON BRINGS THE MAN INTO THE TEXIAN CAMP...
I FOUND ANOTHER RUNAWAY!
EL PRESIDENTE!
EL PRESIDENTE!
EL PRESIDENTE!
EL PRESIDENTE!
EL PRESIDENTE!
HOUSTON WISELY KEEPS THE MEXICAN DICTATOR ALIVE...
ON APRIL 23RD, GOOD NEWS ARRIVES AT THE ROSE FAMILY CAMPSITE...
IT SAYS WE CAN GO HOME, DILUE. THE TEXIAN ARMY HAS DEFEATED THE MEXICAN ARMY...
WHAT DOES IT SAY, FATHER?

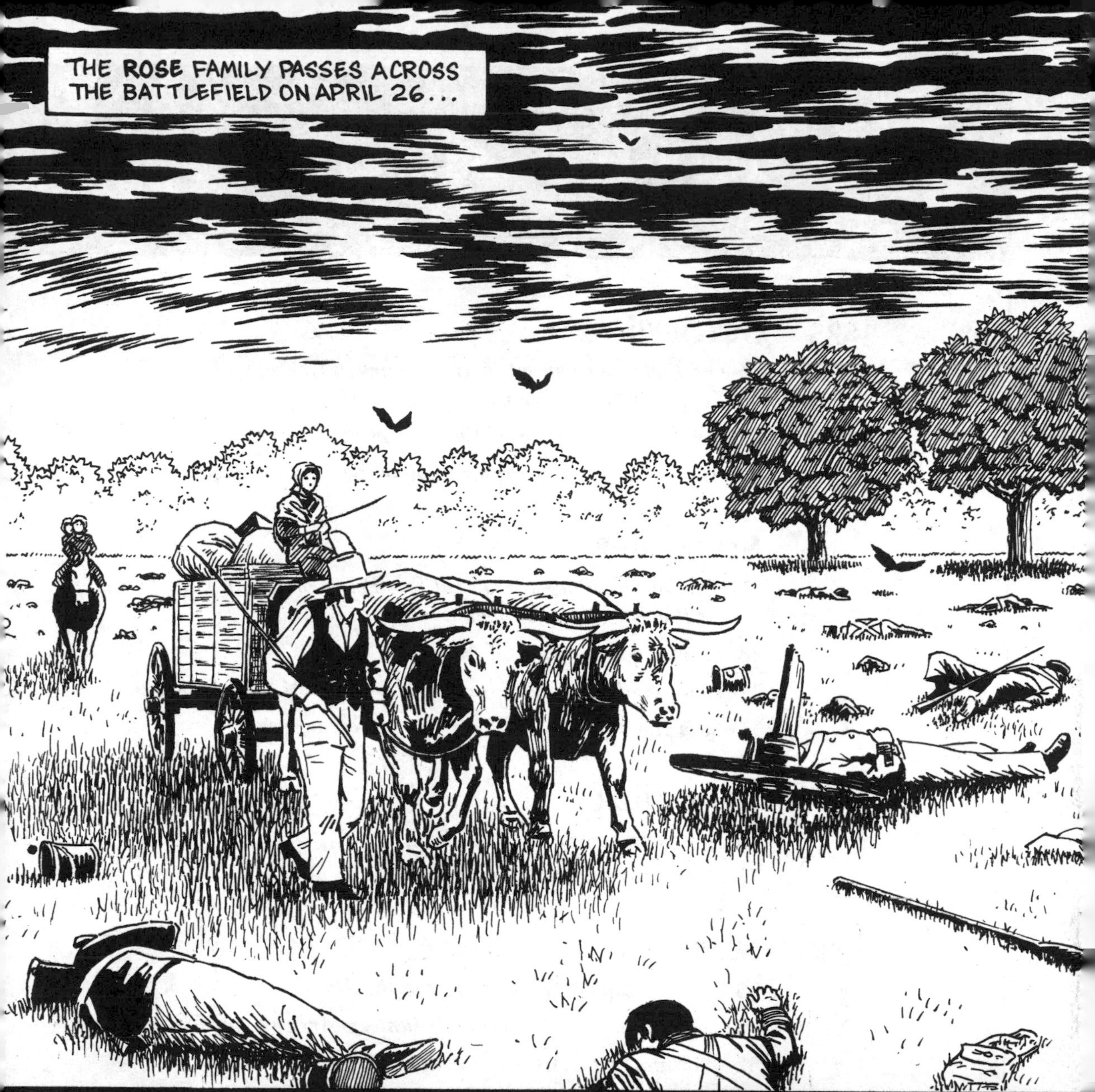
THE ROSE FAMILY PASSES ACROSS THE BATTLEFIELD ON APRIL 26...

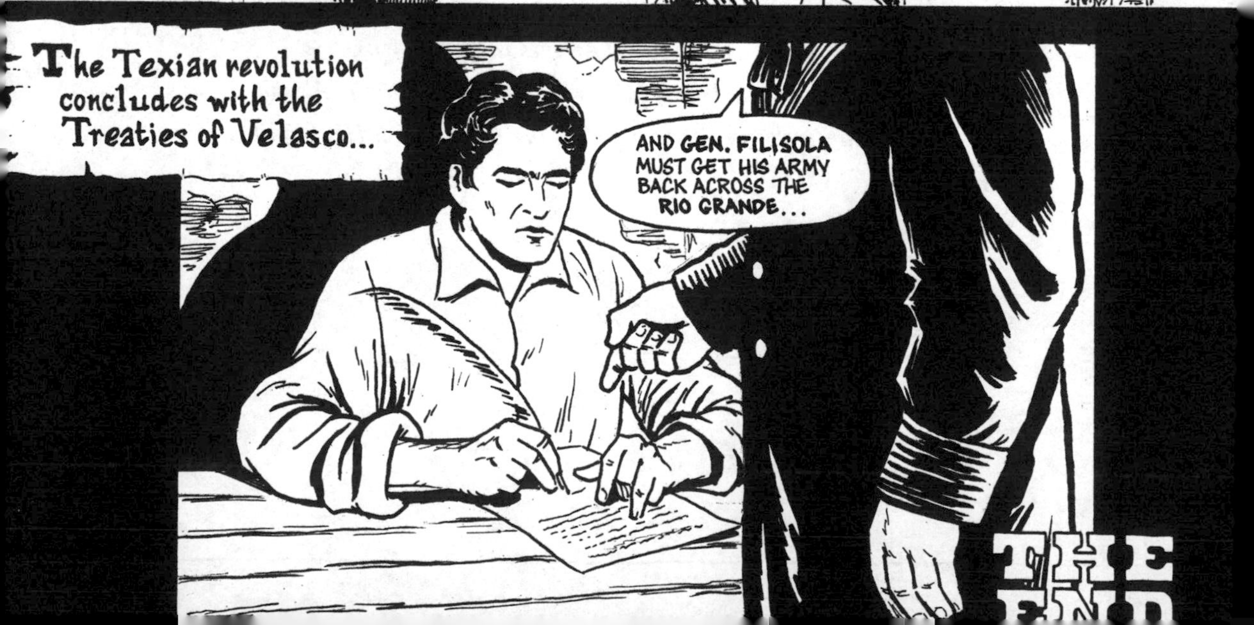
The Texian revolution concludes with the Treaties of Velasco...
AND GEN. FILISOLA MUST GET HIS ARMY BACK ACROSS THE RIO GRANDE...
THE END

The Revolution Time Line

1835   **OCTOBER**

2 *Old Eighteen Confront Mexican Army at Gonzales—*
   Texas Revolution Begins

9 *General Martín Perfecto Cos Arrives in Béxar*

24 *Austin's Army of the People Commences Béxar Campaign*

NOVEMBER

1 *3rd Consultation Assembles at San Felipe to Submit Plan*
   for Provisional Government

13 *Provisional Government Approved*

14 *Henry Smith Elected Governor of Provisional Government*

14 *Sam Houston Elected Major General of the Armies*

DECEMBER

10 *Army of the People Capture Béxar*

15 *Santa Anna's Siete Leyes Passed*

1836   **FEBRUARY**

3 *William Barret Travis Arrives at the Alamo*

8 *David Crockett & Tennessee Volunteers Arrive at the Alamo*

12 *William Travis Assumes Command of the*
   Regular Army at the Alamo

23 *Santa Anna's Army Arrives in Béxar*

23 *William Travis Moves the Garrison into the Alamo*

23 *Gregorio Esparza Enters the Alamo with His Family*

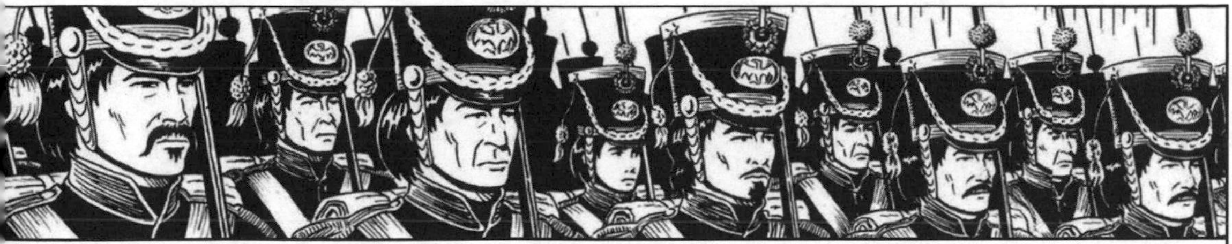

1836
(continued)

MARCH

1 *The Gonzales Mounted Rangers Enter the Alamo*

1 *Independence Convention Meets at Washington-on-the-Brazos*

2 *Texas Declares its Independence*

6 *The Alamo Garrison Falls*

13 *Deaf Smith Finds Alamo Survivors on the Road to Gonzales*

13 *General Houston Evacuates Gonzales—The Runaway Scrape Begins*

14 *The Pleasant W. Rose Family is Warned by a Houston Courier to Flee Their Farm*

19 *Mexican Army Surrounds Colonel James Fannin's Men at Coleto Creek*

20 *Fannin Surrenders to General José de Urrea at Coleto Creek*

26 *Santa Anna Issues Orders to Execute the Goliad Prisoners*

27 *Goliad Massacre—Francisca Panchita Alavez Saves Benjamin Franklin Hughes*

31 *General Houston Retreats to Groces Plantation to Drill the Texas Army*

APRIL

11 *The Twin Sisters Arrive at Groces Plantation*

16 *The Texas Army Reaches Abraham's Gate and Takes the Road to Harrisburg*

20 *The Texas and Mexican Armies Are Both in Place at San Jacinto*

21 *General Houston Orders Deaf Smith to Burn Vince's Bridge*

21 *The Texas Army Attacks the Mexican Camp at 4 P.M.*

22 *Santa Anna Captured by Joel Robison*

MAY

14 *Treaty of Velasco Signed*

DECEMBER

19 *Republic of Texas Passes Legislation Setting Southern and Western Boundaries of its Territory*

TEXAS TALES ILLUSTRATED

———— ⊷∽∞∽⊶ ————

THE REVOLUTION

The Gonzales Mounted Rangers

Between November 1835 and March 1836, the provisional government (The General Council) governed Texas. On November 24, 1835, the council passed an act authorizing the establishment of three companies of rangers under the command of Major Robert McAlpin Williamson (Three-Legged Willie). The companies would each comprise fifty-six men.

In February 1836, the council found that only two companies had been raised and those did not carry the full complement of men. As a result, the council proposed that two new companies be raised in Gonzales and Milam. Further, the council decided that as soon as twenty-eight men were raised, the company could select a lieutenant to lead the unit. By February 23, 1836, twenty-two men comprised the Gonzales Company and even though the unit was short of the twenty-eight man requirement, the company elected Second Lieutenant George Kimble as its leader.

The original twenty-two men ranged in age from sixteen (Galba Fugua) to fifty (Prospect McCoy). One enrollee into the company, John G. King, was allowed to trade places with his son, William Philip King (age fifteen). Kimble's company rode for the Alamo on February 27 with twenty-five men, but only thirteen men from his February 23 muster roll entered the Alamo on March 1, 1836. Most historians believe that eight of Kimble's original twenty-two men were replaced by others or did not make it to the Alamo at all. Kimble picked up seven volunteers along the way to the Alamo. The Gonzales relief force that entered the Alamo on March 1 numbered thirty-two men. All thirty-two perished during the battle.

The Texas Independence Convention

In December 1835, the provisional government (The General Council) called for the convention to meet at Washington-on-the-Brazos. Sixty-two delegates were elected from twenty-five Texas municipalities on February 1, 1836.

The convention began on March 1, 1836, in a small windowless building rented for the delegates by local Washington merchants. The Washington business community used the lure of free rent to move the meeting place from previous consultations at San Felipe. Forty-four delegates presented credentials the first day. Fifty-nine delegates ultimately attended the convention. Three delegates, James Kerr (Jackson), John Linn (Victoria), and Juan Antonio Padilla (Goliad) were unable to attend. Richard Ellis (Red River) was elected convention president. Ellis then appointed a Declaration of Independence committee. George Childress (Milam) chaired the committee.

The Texas Declaration of Independence was written in one day. Most historians believe Childress arrived at the convention with an almost completed draft of the document. Childress cited that the Mexican government under Santa Anna had ceased to provide basic human rights to the citizens of Texas, especially the right of trial by jury (Due Process). The document was approved without debate. Delegates began signing the document on March 3, 1836, officially establishing the Republic of Texas.

On March 4, Sam Houston (Refugio) was elected as Commander-in-Chief of the Texas Army. On March 7, conscription resolutions (The Draft) were passed mustering into service all males between the ages of seventeen and fifty. On March 17, after electing David Gouverneur Burnet as interim president of the new republic, the convention adjourned with the reports of an advancing Mexican army.

Ten signers of the Texas Declaration of Independence were on the battlefield at San Jacinto. They were Sam Houston, Thomas Jefferson Rusk, Dr. Junious Mottley, James Collinsworth, Dr. Thomas J. Gazley, Robert Coleman, William Scates, E.O. Legrand, John W. Bunton, and Andrew Briscoe.

Enrique Esparza

In the late afternoon of February 23, 1836, José María "Gregorio" Esparza, a Tejano soldier in the Plácido Benavides company, brought his wife, Ana Salazar Esparza, his stepdaughter, María de Jesús Castro Esparza, his oldest son, Enrique, and two younger sons, Francisco and Manuel, to the Alamo for protection. Enrique was eight years old at the time of the siege. Sixty-six years later, as the only living survivor of the Alamo, Enrique's recollections were told for the first time in the San Antonio *Light* after being interviewed by Adina de Zavala, granddaughter of the first vice president of the Republic of Texas, Lorenzo de Zavala.

Enrique spent most of his time during the thirteen-day siege in the church with his mother and siblings. One of Enrique's recollections involved a young Anglo boy, about his age, who awoke during the storming of the church. As the boy rose to his feet, he gathered a blanket around his shoulders and was immediately shot and killed by advancing Mexican soldiers.

Enrique's father, Gregorio, was killed during the battle. His uncle, Francisco, fought on the Centralist side. In the battle's aftermath, Francisco obtained permission from Santa Anna to bury Gregorio's body in the local cemetery, San Fernando Campo Santo. Gregorio was the only defender at the Alamo to avoid cremation in the funeral pyres that burned on either side of the Alameda.

Later, Enrique, Francisco, and Manuel moved to Atascosa County to farm and ranch on the land grant given the family for Gregorio's service to the republic. The brothers were responsible for the construction of the church in San Augustine, Texas.

The Angel of Goliad

On Palm Sunday, March 27, 1836, fifteen-year-old Benjamin Franklin Hughes was pulled from a group of Texas prisoners by an officer of the Mexican Army. The prisoners, from James Walker Fannin's command (The Battle of Coleto), were unknowingly marching toward their executions. Hughes recalled years later that a young woman, Madame Captain Alavez (Francisca Panchita Alavez) spoke with General Urrea's wife moments before he was taken from the ranks. Hughes was not the first Texan whose life was spared by her heroic actions. Firsthand narratives reveal she was responsible for saving Dr. Joseph H. Barnard (Goliad/La Bahía), Dr. Jack Shackelford (Goliad/La Bahía), and Rueben R. Brown (San Patricio). Dr. Barnard wrote, "During the time of the massacre (Massacre at La Bahía) she stood in the street, her hair floating, speaking wildly, and abusing the Mexican officers, especially Portilla (José Nicolás de la Portilla). She appeared almost frantic."

Regarding the capture of Major William P. Miller and his men at Copano, Francisca had their ropes removed and provided them water. Dr. Shackelford wrote of Francisca, "I consider it not inappropriate here to mention one female, Pacheta Alevesco, the wife of Captain A. She was indeed an Angel of Mercy— a second Pocahontas. All that she could do to administer to our comfort— 'to pour oil into our wounds'—was done. She had likewise been to Maj. Miller and men, a ministering angel."

Francisca's son, Mathias, told Elena Zamora O'Shea, a King Ranch schoolteacher (1902-1903), that his father was Telesforo Alavéz. Mrs. O'Shea wrote later that she had met Francisca in her nineties. The Angel of Goliad is buried in an unmarked grave on the ranch.

The Recollections of Dilue Rose Harris

In 1900, the recollections of Dilue Rose Harris were published in the quarterly journal of the Texas State Historical Association (Vol. IV, *Southwestern Historical Quarterly*). Dilue's reminiscences were combined with accounts kept by her father in a journal (Dr. Pleasant W. Rose). The journal offers readers an intense, vivid pictorial of the "Runaway Scrape," the scramble by Texas colonists to the Louisiana border and protection in the United States (Taking the Sabine Chute), and is dated 1833-1837.

The Rose family farm was located on the east bank of the Brazos River (Fort Bend County), west of present-day Houston. The Roses were friends of Colonel William B. Travis. After hearing of his death and the deaths of his men at the Alamo, they began making plans to flee Santa Anna's approaching army (Santanistas). Mrs. Rose's brother, James Wells, prepared to join Houston's army. Dilue recounted how her mother sewed James two striped hickory shirts, while she (Dilue) melted lead in a pot to be used in the molding of bullets for her uncle. In mid-March, the Rose family left home, hauling their possessions on a sled pulled by a yoke of oxen. Upon reaching the San Jacinto River crossing, they became part of an exodus of five thousand people. The ferry crossing took three days.

Dilue's account of the Trinity River crossing provides a powerful chronicle of the hardships placed on the fleeing farmers. A rising Trinity ran over its banks stranding the family for several hours. During their crossing, one of Dilue's younger sisters, sick when their journey began, went into convulsions and died later. The Roses buried the child in Liberty, Texas.

On April 22, while proceeding to the Sabine, a courier named McDermot arrived with a dispatch from Gen. Houston. He told the colonists that Santa Anna's army had been defeated at San Jacinto and it was safe to return to their homes.

The Twin Sisters

During the Texas struggle for independence, the citizens of Cincinnati, Ohio, furnished Sam Houston's army with two artillery pieces that later became known as the "Twin Sisters."

According to the *Bulletin of the Historical and Philosophical Society of Ohio,* (Volume 10, 1952, written by E.N. Clopper) on November 17, 1835, a group of Cincinnatians, Friends of Texas, met in the courthouse to consider the reports of ward committees on giving aid to Texas insurgents. The Ohio gentleman who presided over this meeting was Nicholas Clopper, also the brother-in-law of David Burnet, who would later serve as president of the Republic of Texas. Also present at the meeting was a former United States legislator, Robert T. Lytle, who offered several resolutions, one being, "That we approve and recommend to the citizens of this meeting a plan by which the citizens of Texas, shall be supplied through their agent, Mr. Smith (William Bryan Smith), by our contributions with such an amount of hollow ware as he (Smith) may deem sufficient, to contain other provisions, by which they shall be filled, according to his judgment and sound discretion." The resolution was unanimously accepted.

The cannon were manufactured at the Eagle Foundry (also referred to in some documents as Eagle Iron Works) in Cincinnati and later shipped down the Mississippi to New Orleans to Galveston to Harrisburg and finally to the Texian Army at Groce's Plantation. Miles Greenwood and Joseph Webb owned the Eagle Foundry. The "Twins" were passed through customs as "hollow ware", which was the customs designation for glassware and bottles. The fact that United States customs allowed the pieces through is indicative of Andrew Jackson's "neutrality" during the conflict.

In the *Bulletin of the Historical and Philosophical Society of Ohio* (Volume 11, 1953, written by E. N. Clopper), Clopper offers a letter excerpt from Hugh C. Mitchell of Washington, D.C., written by his grandmother, Elizabeth Rice. Elizabeth's father, Dr. Charles W. Rice, joined the Texas Navy in 1836. Elizabeth and her twin sister, Eleanor, were aboard the same steamboat as the cannon in April 1836. All arrived in Texas together. Legend has it that Elizabeth and Eleanor were taught a short presentation speech to formally present the cannon to Texas . . . and from that time on the cannon were referred to as the "Twin Sisters." Elizabeth also wrote, "I have not made much noise in this world, but my Namesake did."

Juan Nepomuceno Seguín

Only one company of Houston's assembled troops at San Jacinto were composed of native Texians (Tejanos). These men were under the command of thirty-year-old Captain Juan Seguín. Seguín's company participated in the ouster of General Cos from San Antonio in December 1835 and entered the Alamo with Travis and others in February 1836. Seguín left the Alamo as a courier on February 25 escaping the fate of seven of his men. After the battle, it fell to Seguín to inter the ashes of the heroes of the Alamo.

At San Jacinto, Seguín and his company were attached to Sidney Sherman's Second Regiment and wore white pasteboard in their hats to distinguish themselves from enemy combatants during the battle. Seguín served in the Second, Third, and Fourth Congress of the new republic as a senator, he was the only Tejano Texian in the legislature. In 1841, Seguín was elected Mayor of San Antonio. The city of Seguin in Guadalupe County, Texas, is named after Juan Nepomuceno Seguín.

The San Jacinto Battlefield

The battlefield, eight miles north of New Washington, was located on a prairie within a league of land owned by Margaret (Peggy) McCormick. Buffalo Bayou bordered the prairie on the northwest, San Jacinto Bay on the northeast, a large lake (Peggy's Lake) on the southeast, and surrounding marshland. Eight miles southwest of the prairie was Vince's Bridge, which led to Harrisburg and provided the only escape route for either army.

Peggy and her sons fled their ranch in late April as Santa Anna's troops approached. Days after the battle, Peggy returned home to find her ranch pilfered and her land strewn with the bodies of Mexican soldiers. She confronted Sam Houston and Santa Anna demanding that one or both men bury the dead. Both refused. Peggy and her sons buried what bodies they could. Peggy died in a suspicious fire in her home in 1854. Speculation was that the widow, who had once owned one of the largest cattle herds in Harris County, had been robbed and possibly murdered before the fire was set.

Mike McCormick, who had warned President Burnet of the approaching Col. Almonte at New Washington, drowned in 1875 near the spot where his father had drowned in 1824.

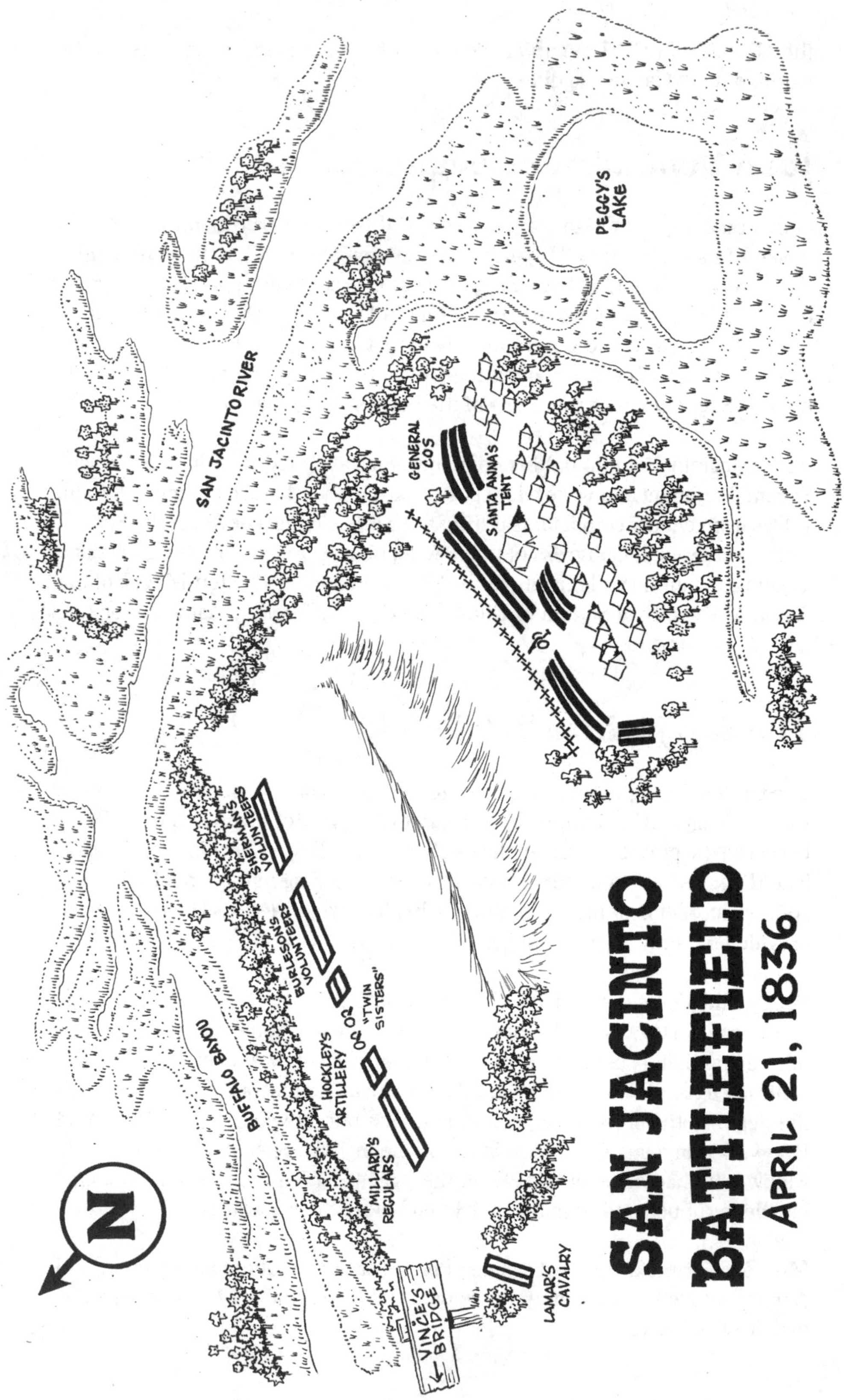
SAN JACINTO
BATTLEFIELD
APRIL 21, 1836
SAN JACINTO RIVER
PEGGY'S LAKE
GENERAL COS
SANTA ANNA'S TENT
SHERMAN'S VOLUNTEERS
BURLESON'S VOLUNTEERS
HOCKLEY'S ARTILLERY
"TWIN SISTERS"
MILLARD'S REGULARS
BUFFALO BAYOU
VINCE'S BRIDGE
LAMAR'S CAVALRY
N

The Treaties of Velasco

FIRST TREATY OF VELASCO

ARTICLE 1. General Antonio López de Santa Anna agrees that he will not take up arms, nor will he exercise his influence to cause them to be taken up, against the people of Texas during the present war of Independence.

ARTICLE 2. All hostilities between the Mexican and Texian troops will cease immediately, both on land and water.

ARTICLE 3. The Mexican troops will evacuate the Territory of Texas, passing to the other side of the Río Grande del Norte.

ARTICLE 4. The Mexican Army in its retreat shall not take the property of any person without his consent and just indemnification, using only such articles as may be necessary for its subsistence in cases where the owner may not be present, and remitting to the Commander of the Army of Texas, or to the Commissioners to be appointed for the adjustment of such matters, an account of the value of the property consumed, the place where taken, and the name of the owner, if it can be ascertained.

ARTICLE 5. That all private property, including cattle, horses, negro slaves, or indentured persons, of whatever denomination, that may have been captured by any portion of the Mexican Army, or may have taken refuge in the said army since the commencement of the late invasion, shall be restored to the Commander of the Texian Army, or to such other persons as may be appointed by the Government of Texas to receive them.

ARTICLE 6. The troops of both armies will refrain from coming into contact with each other, and to this end the Commander of the Army of Texas will be careful not to approach within a shorter distance of the Mexican army than five leagues.

ARTICLE 7. The Mexican Army shall not make any other delay on its march than that which is necessary to take up their hospitals, baggage, etc., and to cross the rivers: any delay not necessary to these purposes to be considered an infraction of this agreement.

ARTICLE 8. By express, to be immediately dispatched, this agreement shall be sent to General Vincent Filisola and to General T. J. Rusk, Commander of the Texian Army, its order that they may be apprised of its stipulations, and to this end they will exchange engagements to comply with the same.

ARTICLE 9. That all Texian prisoners now in possession of the Mexican Army or its authorities be forthwith released and furnished with free passports to return to their homes, in consideration of which a corresponding number of Mexican prisoners, rank and file, now in possession of the Government of Texas, shall be immediately released. The remainder of the Mexican prisoners that continue in possession of the Government of Texas to be treated with due humanity; any extraordinary comforts that may be furnished them to be at the charge of the Government of Mexico.

ARTICLE 10. General Antonio López of Santa Anna will be sent to Vera Cruz as soon as it shall be deemed proper.

SECRET TREATY OF VELASCO

Port of Velasco, May 14th, 1836. Antonio López de Santa Anna, General-in-Chief of the Army of Operations, and President of the Republic of Mexico, before the Government established in Texas, solemnly pledges himself to fulfill the stipulations contained in the following articles, so far as concerns himself:

ARTICLE 1. He will not take up arms, nor cause them to be taken up, against the people of Texas, during the present war for Independence.

ARTICLE 2. He will give his orders that in the shortest time the Mexican troops may leave the Territory of Texas.

ARTICLE 3. He will so prepare matters in the Cabinet of Mexico, that the mission that may be sent thither by the Government of Texas may be well received, and that by means of negotiations all differences may be settled, and the Independence that has been declared by the Convention may be acknowledged.

ARTICLE 4. A treaty of comity, amity, acid limits, will be established between Mexico and Texas, the territory of the latter not to extend beyond the Río Bravo del Norte.

ARTICLE 5. The present return of General Santa Anna to Vera Cruz being indispensable for the purpose of effecting his solemn engagements, the Government of Texas will provide for his immediate embarkation for said port.

ARTICLE 6. This instrument being obligatory off one part, as well as off the other, will be signed in duplicate, remaining folded and sealed until the negotiations shall have been concluded, when it will be restored to His Excellency General Santa Anna no use of it to be made before that time, unless there should be an infraction by either of the contracting parties. Antonio López de Santa Anna. David G. Burnet James Collingsworth, Secretary of State. Bailey Hardeman, Secretary of the Treasury. P. W. Grayson, Attorney-General.

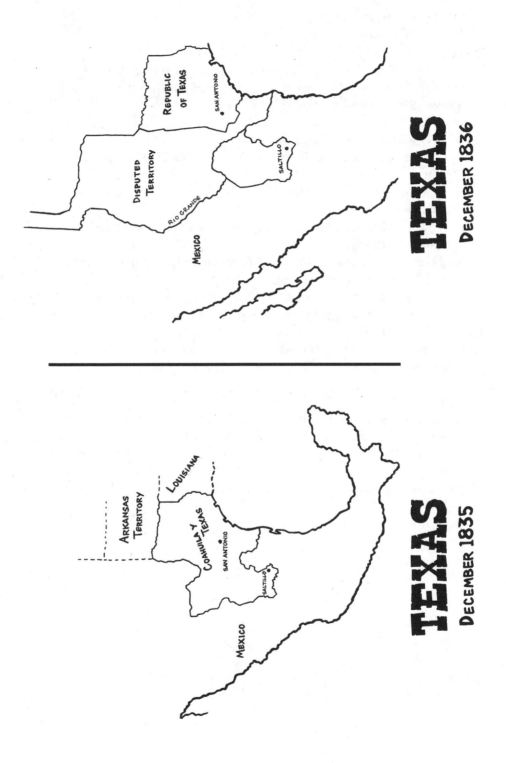

TEXAS

DECEMBER 1836

REPUBLIC OF TEXAS

SAN ANTONIO

DISPUTED TERRITORY

RIO GRANDE

SALTILLO

MEXICO

TEXAS

DECEMBER 1835

ARKANSAS TERRITORY

LOUISIANA

COAHUILA Y TEXAS

SAN ANTONIO

SALTILLO

MEXICO

SELECTED BIBLIOGRAPHY

Books:

Duval, John C. Early *Times in Texas, or the Adventures of Jack Dobell.* Edited by Mabel Major and Rebecca W. Smith. Lincoln: University of Nebraska Press, 1986.

Exley, Jo Ella Powell, ed. *Texas Tears and Texas Sunshine.* College Station: Texas A&M University Press, 1985.

Hardin, Stephen. *Texian Iliad, A Military History of the Texas Revolution.* Austin: University of Texas Press, 1994.

Huffines, Alan. *Blood of Noble Men, The Alamo Siege & Battle.* Austin, TX: Eakin Press, 1999.

Jackson, Jack. *The Alamo: An Epic Told from Both Sides.* Austin: Paisano Graphics, 2002.

Lemon, Mark. *The Illustrated Alamo 1836: A Photographic Journey.* Buffalo Gap, TX: State House Press, 1998.

Moore, Stephen. *Eighteen Minutes, The Battle of San Jacinto and the Texas Independence Campaign.* Dallas: Republic of Texas Press, 2004.

Tolbert, Frank. *The Day of San Jacinto.* New York: McGraw-Hill, 1959.

Winders, Bruce. *Sacrificed at the Alamo, Tragedy and Triumph in the Texas Revolution,* Buffalo Gap, TX: State House Press, 2004.

Internet:

McKeehan, Wallace. "War of Independence 1832-1836," 1997-2004, *Sons of DeWitt Colony Texas,* http://www.tamu.edu/ccbn/dewitt/independcon.htm

Pamphlets:

Clopper, E.N. *Bulletin of the Historical and Philosophical Society of Ohio,* Volume 10, 1952.